THE
WARRIOR
IS SILENT

THE
WARRIOR
IS SILENT

Martial Arts and the Spiritual Path

SCOTT SHAW, PH.D.

Inner Traditions
Rochester, Vermont

Inner Traditions International
One Park Street
Rochester, Vermont 05767
www.gotoit.com

Library of Congress Cataloging-in-Publication Data
Shaw, Scott, 1958–
        The warrior is silent : martial arts and the spiritual path / Scott Shaw.
               p.   cm.
        Includes bibliographical references (p.) and index.
        ISBN 0-89281-668-6 (pbk. : alk. paper)
        1. Martial arts—Religious aspects.   2. Martial arts—Religious aspects—
        History.   3. Spiritual life.   I. Title.
        GV1102.7.R44S53 1998
        796.8—dc21   98-9214
                        CIP
Printed and bound in Canada

10 9 8 7 6 5 4 3 2 1

Distributed to the book trade in Canada by Publishers Group West (PGW),
     Toronto
Distributed to the book trade in the United Kingdom by Deep Books, London
Distributed to the book trade in Australia by Gemcraft Books, Burwood
Distributed to the book trade in New Zealand by Tandem Press, Auckland
Distributed to the book trade in South Africa by Alternative Books, Ferndale

Contents

Introduction

Since the dawn of humankind, physical conflict has defined many of the world's political, cultural, and economic transformations. Acts of war began long before recorded history. In both ancient and modern physical confrontations, the motivating factor is almost always that the people involved have different ideologies. Whether or not these differing mind-sets have proven to be *just* is a matter for historians to determine. Nonetheless, warfare has remained a focal point of human evolution.

Early in our recorded history, warfare began to take on a formalized quality because the participants were looking for ways to increase their chances of emerging victorious in battle. The first literary work detailing the strategies of war has come to be known as *Sun Tzu: The Art of War*, authored in approximately 300 B.C.E. during the Warring States period of Chinese history (403–221 B.C.E.). This text details a strategic approach to how the warrior general and his army should enter into battle.

The ancient Chinese militarists were the first to practice a prescribed, formal warfare. The first formalized group of soldiers to add a spiritual understanding to their combat ideology, however, was the Hwa Rang (Flowering Youth) warriors of the Korean Peninsula kingdom of Silla during the fifth century C.E. The Hwa Rang warriors not only trained their bodies in all forms of known martial combat, but also embraced a Buddhist ideology. With this combination of disciplines they brought warfare to a new level of spiritual understanding.

Because of the close proximity of the Korean Peninsula to the island nation of Japan, many cultural transmissions have taken place between the two since around the third century C.E. Through these interactions, not only were Chinese statesmanship and medical practices transmitted to Japan, but the religion of Buddhism was also introduced from Korea to Japan, in the sixth century C.E. These cultural disseminations eventually gave rise to the famed Japanese samurai tradition, which ultimately ushered spiritual warfare into the modern era.

As methods of warfare have continued to advance, hand-to-hand applications of combat have been replaced by weapons of mass destruction, rendering obsolete the need for advanced interactive personal self-defense among soldiers. The martial arts, once the mainstay of Asian warfare, have given way to bullets and bombs.

In recent decades, the martial arts systems practiced throughout Asia have reached a level of cultural acceptance. Having moved away from being the sole property of the military aristocracy, martial arts training has become widely accessible. With this change comes the refinement of martial arts techniques to a new level, at which the struggle for life or death is no longer the motivator. Instead, people now study martial arts for self-defense, enriched health, for physical and mental refinement, and to form a more conscious relationship between their body, mind, and spirit.

Today the martial artist finds herself practicing and mastering an art she may never need to use in actual physical combat. Nonetheless, many instructors continue to teach the martial arts as very physically aggressive systems of self-defense, with little thought for the inner growth of the individual student. For this reason, modern martial artists who desire more than simple physical aptitude in combat must step forward on their own and explore the spiritual realms of the martial arts, not only to become more complete martial artists, but also to become more whole as individuals.

For the modern martial arts practitioner to expand into the spiritual realms of the martial arts is a step-by-step process. The first level of study involves the practitioner coming to a clear, perceptive, psychologically awakened attitude toward the physical and nonphysical worlds. This process is initially accomplished by training in replacing nonproductive thought patterns with conscious, socially interactive methods of relating with the external world and oneself. Once this level of understanding has been reached, the martial artist can move forward to the next level of spiritual evolution, that of developing a very precise and clarified focus of consciousness. The practitioner achieves this by performing the ancient practices of controlled breathing and meditation that have been handed down by monks for centuries. From these meditation techniques, the martial artist comes to develop a one-pointedness of spiritual purpose that is not experienced by the average individual. Through continued meditation practice, the martial artist comes to understand and interact with the unceasing energy of the universe,

known as *ki* in Japanese, *qui* or *chi* in Chinese. This understanding leads the practitioner to the next level of refined martial understanding, that of forming a conscious link between the body, mind, and the positive spiritual energy of the universe.

Martial artists who progress through these levels of study come to understand that the perfection of advanced combative techniques is not the sole purpose of martial arts training. Instead, to the conscious martial artist, physical fighting techniques are based on an enlightened understanding of the constant movement of energy in the universe.

When all of these levels of study and practice have been mastered, a new and complete spiritual warrior emerges. This warrior is able to view and interact with all human beings and the universe with the enlightened attitude of the ancients. With that view, the spiritual warrior moves to the level of an enlightened being: at one with all, at war with no one, in constant harmony with the never ceasing movement of positive universal energy.

1

THE HISTORICAL FOUNDATIONS OF THE MARTIAL ARTS

Warfare has been practiced and refined since the dawn of humankind. Until the sixth century, the cultivation of martial skills was based predominately on winning the battle. During the sixth century C.E., however, a group of Buddhist monk-warriors, known as the Hwa Rang, emerged in the Korean Peninsula kingdom of Silla. These highly trained Buddhist warriors set the stage for the evolution of martial arts from being simply refined acts of violence to a pathway to spiritual enlightenment.

Those who are familiar with the nonviolent nature of Buddhism may find the notion of Buddhist warriors hard to grasp. It should be understood, however, that when Buddhism first came from India across the Tibetan Plateau to China and then to Korea, the political regimes of these regions were based on a Confucian doctrine that elevated the state to a level of reverence. Chinese and Korean societies, on the whole, had not yet achieved the metaphysically advanced mind-set already present in India. Therefore, the various established kingdoms possessed the desire for continual expansionism, believing that it was their right and, in fact, destiny to defeat their geographical neighbors.

4

As Buddhism was initially embraced by the rural inhabitants of these aristocracies, if the religion came to be approved of by the royal court it was most often as a method for the king to establish greater control over his subjects rather than as a desire for spiritual development.

The Buddhism originally practiced in China and Korea was not the highly evolved school of meditative thought that is in evidence today. The advancement of Buddhism was brought about by practicing monastics, who, through years of seclusion, developed the various meditation techniques that have come to be the basis of the Buddhist meditative tradition.

CHINA

The foundations of the spiritual warriors can be traced to ancient China. Religious history in China dates back to the Xia Dynasty, which existed from approximately 2200 until 1600 B.C.E. During this period of Chinese history, archeological fragments of oracle bones suggest that religious human sacrifices took place. In approximately 1600 B.C.E., the Shang Dynasty arose in northern China. The Shang had a strict system of state loyalty in association with reverence for village elders and priests of the dominant tribal religion. This belief system of duty to the government and devotion to the religious hierarchy has permeated the Chinese mind-set since that period. The Zhou Dynasty, 1027 B.C.E., followed the overthrow of the Shang. Between 771 and 770 B.C.E., an uprising against the Zhou authority took place and dissidents within the Zhou nobility left the confines of the kingdom and allied themselves with nomadic tribes from the north. The period of social chaos in China that followed is known as the Warring States period (403–221 B.C.E.). During this period several independent Chinese political states formed. The three states that formed in the southern region of China, Ch'u, Wu, and Yueh, would have the most important role in the forming of Chinese culture.

TAOISM

During the Warring States period several of the most profound written works defining Chinese culture were created, including: The *Tao Te Ching*, *The Inner Chapters*, *The Confucian Doctrines*, *Sun Tzu: The Art of War*, and *The Huang Ti Nei Ching Su Wen* (*The Yellow Emperor's Classic of Internal Medicine*). These are among the first written works to truly set the stage for the development of the spiritual martial arts.

One of the most influential schools of philosophical thought to emerge from China, especially in regard to the martial arts, is that of Taoism. Taoism was first established in the Chinese state of Ch'u in the Yangtze Valley around 1000 B.C.E. Although the foundation of Taoism is traced to this period, three major documents of Taoist ideology appear to have been written during the Warring States period of Chinese history. The authors of these works were Lao-tzu, Kung Fu-tzu—or as he is more commonly known, Confucius—and Chuang Tzu.

Lao-tzu

The name Lao-tzu can be literally translated as "Old Boy." This translation is a bit too literal for its colloquial meaning to be understood. In English, the name, or more probably the title, he came to be known by is more precisely translated as "Old Master."

According to legend, Lao-tzu was the keeper of the royal archives at Loyang, the Ch'u capital. Few details of his life are known; he was a reclusive wise man, reluctant to found a school and gather a following. Lao-tzu supposedly became despondent over the con-

tinued wars that took place during his lifetime, and as a result, he left the Ch'u capital and wandered out into the wilderness to die. As he was leaving he was persuaded by a gatekeeper to write down his thoughts for posterity. This he did, producing the renowned Taoist work, the *Tao Te Ching*.

The Tao Te Ching teaches that everything begins in nothingness and ultimately returns to nothingness. In Chinese this nothingness is known by the word wu, and the returning to nothingness is referred to as fu. Taoist understanding teaches that everything witnessed in physical life exists in an ongoing cycle from nonaction to action, returning to its ultimate essence in nonaction. As such, the spiritual warrior consciously embraces nonaction.

Nonaction is not the negative response to action. Instead, mindful nonaction is understood to be the pathway to suchness (the uninhibited encountering of cosmic understanding). For this reason the spiritual warrior accepts the inevitable changes of life, witnessing them but not becoming bound by them. She willingly performs the necessary tasks of life, knowing that they only express the transient nature of this physical world, ultimately leading one to return to the great ethereal abyss.

Kung Fu-tzu

Kung Fu-tzu (Confucius) was another personage who laid the foundations of Taoism and certain aspects of Chinese culture on the whole. Kung Fu-tzu was a descendant of Shang kings, believed to have been a younger contemporary of Lao-tzu.

Kung Fu-tzu's contribution had a less dramatic effect upon the overall growth and development of mystical Taoism than did Lao-tzu's. Kung Fu-tzu's philosophy included the worship of heaven and was full of magical rites to invoke and please the Chinese gods. He also wrote of the divine qualities of loyalty to the state and servitude to the kings and their court. To the Chinese public, Kung Fu-tzu's work is the most representative of practiced Taoism. From the time of feudal Chinese society and onward, his writings have been used to define Chinese statesmanship and have directly influenced later generations of Chinese, Korean, and Japanese political regimes.

Chuang Tzu

Chuang Tzu was the third individual whose written work contributed substantially to the shaping of early Taoism. It is believed that Chuang Tzu was an official in the Lacquer Garden of Meng in Honan Province around the fourth century B.C.E. Chuang Tzu took the ideology of Taoism laid down by Lao-tzu and further defined the doctrines of mystical Taoism using logic as a basis.

Chuang Tzu's written work is generally referred to as *The Inner Chapters*. The work, which is very literary in style, metaphorically represents how a Taoist should encounter the world.

Chuang Tzu's writing is both religious and mystical. It illustrates the way in which an individual should encounter every aspect of life, making each action a sacred movement. To the spiritual warrior, this means that each movement leads one toward a better understanding of oneself and the divine. Thus, no action should ever be taken without complete presence of mind.

Inspired by the teachings of Lao-tzu and Chuang Tzu, Taoist sages established a tradition of going to live in retreat. The earliest Taoists often led solitary lives in remote reaches of China—oftentimes living in mountain caves. They spent their lives in meditation and lived in harmony with nature.

YIN AND YANG

The concept of yin and yang, *um* and *yang* in Korean and *omoto yo* and *ura* in

Yin and Yang

in each positive occurrence there is a hint of the negative, just as in in each negative event there is the essence of positive. Thus, good and bad are only a perception or point of view. This is illustrated in the yin and yang symbol by a small dot of white on the black side and a small dot of black on the white side.

The spiritual warrior always seeks a balance between the yin and the yang in life. It is believed that if one is out of balance with yin and yang, illness and misfortune occur. People who live in harmony with the world maintain a conscious balance between yin and yang. When pain and suffering occur, they examine the events in their lives that instigated the pain, realign their directions, and then move forward on paths of harmony.

The human body is the vessel for communication with the universe. As such, people who have harmonized the yin and yang elements of their bodies are naturally in tune with the energies of the universe. All events in this universe—whether they are viewed as positive or negative—are preceded by a set of signs or indications; those who possess a conscious balance of yin and yang are open to taking notice of these indicators. The only time they are surprised by physical or ethereal events is when

Japanese, dates as far back as the eighth century B.C.E. in China. The understanding of a universal duality is one of the most elemental of Asian traditions.

The general idea of yin and yang is based on the notion that all life exists in a balance between active and passive, feminine and masculine, day and night, light and heavy, and hot and cold energies. The symbol of yin and yang depicts this balance (see illustration above).

The symbol of yin and yang is circular, like the Earth. Additionally, life is a cyclical path: when we are born we emerge from the great abyss and when we die we return to it.

During our life our physical being experiences the positive and negative events of this world. As we refine our consciousness we come to perceive that they have allowed themselves to become out of tune with their bodies and the energies prevalent in nature.

NEI CHING

The *Huang Ti Nei Ching Su Wen (The Yellow Emperor's Classic of Internal Medicine)*, commonly referred to as the *Nei Ching*, was the first written text to present ki (chi in Chinese), or internal energy, and its interrelationship with the human body. In the *Nei Ching*, ki is described as the omnipresent universal energy that nourishes and sustains all life.

The *Nei Ching* is written in the form of a dialogue on the subject of healing between the Yellow Emperor, Huang-ti, and his minister, Chi-po. Huang-ti was a mythological ruler of China, said to have lived from 2697 to 2599 B.C.E. Although Chinese folklore claims the *Nei Ching* was written during the life of Huang-ti, the text was actually written in approximately 300 B.C.E.

The *Nei Ching* not only describes ki, it gives extensive details on the functions of the human body. For medical practitioners and metaphysicians of that period to have conceived and written this text was an incredible accomplishment. Along with a relatively correct description of the ana-

tomy of the human body, the *Nei Ching* included the first explanation of blood circulation. The revelation of blood circulation and its role in the human body was described in the Nei Ching two thousand years before European medical scientists discovered it.

The text also describes how ki circulation in the human body is directed by invisible circulation channels known as meridians. Each meridian is named for the major organ or bodily function it effects. Along these meridians are precise access points that allow a trained individual to stimulate the flow of ki, thus nourishing and healing the body. A highly trained martial artist can access these pressure points in a specific manner and thereby hinder the flow of ki in an attacking opponent.

The spiritual warrior studies the flow of ki in the body. With this knowledge he is not only able to defend himself in combat, by striking ki pressure points, but he is also able to heal himself and others in case of physical or mental illness.

SUN TZU

During the same period of Chinese history, seven military classics were written by military leaders. *Sun Tzu*, commonly known as *The Art of War*, has by far gained the most exposure in recent times. This text is China's oldest and most profound military treatise, and it has played an elemental role in military strategy throughout Asian history. It was studied and used extensively by the nations of Korea and Japan in the years of their early military and political development.

The Art of War is a compilation of the military strategies of Sun Wu, a Chinese military leader who lived around 500 B.C.E. In this book he details military strategies and tactical procedures for leaders of armies. Although this work is ancient and profound, it only skirts the implications of mystical understanding. Therefore its usage is limited to tactical maneuvering as opposed to enlightened reasoning.

BUDDHISM

Buddhism, based on the teachings of the wandering Indian renunciate Siddhartha Gautama, came to China in the first century C.E. Siddhartha Gautama was born in 560 B.C.E. in Lumbini, northern India, near present-day Nepal. His father was head of the Shakya clan, and Gautama lived the sheltered life of a prince. According to Buddhist legend, he witnessed sickness, death, poverty, and sorrow for the first time when he was twenty-nine years old. The experience of human suffering drove Prince Siddhartha on a quest to find the remedy for the pain of existence. He lived the life of a *sadhu*, a wandering ascetic, for a time, finding no ultimate answers. After six years of trials and frustration, he sat down under a bodhi tree in Bodh Gaya, India, near Varanasi, and refused to get up until he reached enlightenment. After forty-nine days he rose, an enlightened being. The Sanskrit word *Buddha* means "One who has awakened." After his enlightenment, Siddhartha Gautama roamed India as a lecturing holy man, gathering many disciples until his death in 480 B.C.E. from food poisoning, at the age of eighty.

In most modern accounts, Siddhartha Gautama is commonly referred to as the Buddha. He was, however, by no means the only Buddha. According to the Pali text *The Mahavadana Sutra*, there were twenty-four buddhas existing before Siddhartha Gautama. Additionally, it is understood by Buddhist practitioners that buddhahood is attainable by those who seek enlightenment. Thus, there are many buddhas who have lived since Gautama. He is referred to as the Shakyamuni Buddha. This means "the silent Buddha from the clan of Shakya."

Shakyamuni Buddha explained his enlightened understanding with the premise of the Four Noble Truths:

1. All beings are bound by karma (the law of cause and effect) and, thereby, are subject to suffering.
2. The cause of suffering is desire.
3. The chain of suffering can be broken by obtaining enlightenment.
4. Enlightenment is obtained by following the path of Dharma.

In addition to the Four Noble Truths, a core Buddhist teaching is that of the Eightfold Path, which consists of eight precepts that lead an individual to enlightenment:

1. Right View
2. Right Intention
3. Right Speech
4. Right Conduct
5. Right Livelihood
6. Right Effort
7. Right Mindfulness
8. Right Concentration

Buddhism spread from India to Nepal to Tibet, and then on to China in the first century C.E. By that time strongly defined religious and philo- sophic traditions already existed in China. Therefore, Buddhism was not readily accepted into the Chinese mind- set. Over time, various Buddhist sects came into existence, and certain kings and kingdoms embraced it; however, Buddhism never took hold on a national level. Instead, it existed alongside indi- genous Chinese religions and was prac- ticed by various groups of monks and ascetics who have kept Buddhism alive in China over the centuries.

The Indian Buddhist monk Batsu, or Fu Tsu, as he is known in Chinese, traveled to China in 495 C.E., as a Buddhist missionary. He was instru- mental in the construction of Shong- shan Monastery in the foothills of the Shongshan Mountains. This monastery served as the location for Indian Buddhist monks who came to translate the scriptures into Chinese.

Bodhidharma

The legendary Buddhist monk Bodhi- dharma (Ta Moo in Chinese or Daruma in Japanese) was born in Kanchipuram, India, near Madras. In 520 C.E. he was sent to China from India by his *guru*, Prajnatara, to relieve the missionary Indian monk, Bodhiruci. Prajnatara was the head of the Sarvastivada sect of Buddhism. The Sarvastivada school practiced a less structured approach than did the other traditional Indian Buddhist schools of the time. Thus, the Sarvastivada ideology was more readily accepted by the Chinese than were the previous schools of Buddhism that had entered China over the preceding five centuries.

Bodhidharma first traveled to the city of Kuang, modern-day Guang-Zhou, where he had an audience with Emperor Wu Ti. He then traveled on to Shongshan (Shao Lin) Monastery to take over the abbotship from Bodhiruci. Upon arrival at the monastery, Bodhidharma found that the monastic life had left the monks weak and in ill health. To remedy their physical condition, he taught them a series of exercises that are believed to have laid the foundation for the development of Chinese martial arts. Some historians believe that the now infamous Shao Lin Temple system of Kung Fu was born from the training given by Bodhidharma to the monks at Shong-shan Monastery.

The study of ancient Sanskrit literature reveals that India possessed a refined system of martial arts early in its recorded history. This system of combat is known as Kalaripayit. *Kalari* means "battlefield" and *prayit* translates as "practice of." The physical and spiritual applications of this system are what formed the basis of the exercises Bodhidharma taught to the monks at Shongshan Temple.

Obviously, formalized combat skills had existed in China long before the arrival of Bodhidharma, however, these fighting techniques were limited to those used by the military. What occurred with the training of the monks was that martial skills were no longer solely in the hands of professional warriors. From this initial introduction, over many centuries, numerous schools of martial arts developed in the Chinese Taoist and Buddhist temples. Each of these schools formalized its own techniques and possessed its own unique understanding of the martial arts. The Chinese martial arts are most commonly referred to as Kung Fu or Tai Chi Chuan, but more properly they are called *Wu Shu*.

While in China, Bodhidharma was instrumental in linking Buddhism to Taoist thought. This joining ultimately formed the tradition known as Ch'an Buddhism, the predecessor to Japanese Zen.

THE SHAO LIN TEMPLE

The infamous Shao Lin Temple has been depicted in recent years as being an ancient center for Chinese martial arts. The Shao Lin Temple style of Kung Fu did not come into formal existence, however, until the late Qing Dynasty (1644–1912 C.E.), long after various styles of Chinese martial arts had become commonly practiced by monks in other Taoist and Buddhist temples.

One reason for its renown is that the Taoist martial art practitioners at the Shao Lin Temple were instrumental in the development of their own system of self-defense, known as Five Animal style. Today many modern martial arts systems of Chinese heritage can draw their lineage from either the Northern or the Southern Shao Lin style. The defining factor between these two systems is that kicks are often utilized in offensive and defensive application in the Northern-based styles, and in the Southern styles, close-in hand-technique fighting is employed.

As China moved into the modern era, the Shao Lin Temple became a very politically oriented institution, especially during its later years. It was used as a training ground for antigovernment revolutionaries just prior to and during the Boxer Rebellion (1898–1900), which witnessed all foreign missionaries and businesspeople driven out of China.

KOREA

Formalized Chinese contact with the Korean Peninsula began in approximately 200 B.C.E., during the Chinese Qui Dynasty (221–206 B.C.E.). This contact was later intensified during the Han Dynasty (207 B.C.E.–220 C.E.) by the placement of Chinese military colonies on the northern Korean Peninsula. Through these contacts, the Korean Peninsula advanced rapidly in agriculture, health science, military strategy, and statesmanship. Taoism, Confucianism, and later, Buddhism, were all introduced into Korea from China.

Due to the advancements on the Korean Peninsula brought about by the introduction of Confucian doctrines, and subsequent growing tribal unities, three Korean tribal kingdoms formed: Silla formed in 57 B.C.E.; Koguryo in 37 B.C.E.; and Paekche in 18 B.C.E. This was the beginning of what became known as the Three Kingdom Period of Korean history.

Buddhism came to the Korean Peninsula state of Koguryo in 372 C.E., in the hands of the Chinese monk Sundo, who was sent from the Chinese state of Ch'in on an official mission by King Fu Chein to introduce Buddhism to the Korean kingdom. The East

Indian monk Malananda arrived via China in the Korean state of Paekche in 384 C.E. and was met with an elaborate welcome from the Paekche royal court. Chinese religious culture and society had been transmitted to the Korean states several centuries before Buddhism was introduced. Thus, when Buddhism was brought to Korea by royal Chinese envoys, it was readily accepted in the Korean royal courts. The Korean state of Silla, however, was the exception to this process. Silla did not readily accept Buddhist doctrine; it held fast to the Confucian aristocratic ideology. In fact, attempts at introducing Buddhism were initially met with open hostility. At the beginning of the fifth century C.E., the Buddhist monk A-do had limited success with the introduction of Buddhist ideology to the Kingdom of Silla; it was marginally accepted by rural people in the outlying regions of the kingdom.

King Pop-hung (514–540 C.E.) came to the throne of Silla after the death of his father King Chi-jung (500–514). During the short reign of King Chi-jung, Silla experienced great advances in agricultural and cultural development. As the population of the kingdom was content, the kingdom not only began to expand militaristically against its neighboring kingdoms on

the Korean Peninsula, by the order of King Pop-hung the kingdom embraced Buddhism as well.

Buddhism had been practiced by the common populous of Silla for at least a century before its acceptance by the royal court. It was introduced into the royal house by the monk Won-pyo (502–557), who came from the southern Chinese state of Liang. King Pop-hung was so taken by Buddhism that he was forced to battle against the Silla aristocracy, who attempted to have him assassinated when he decided to have the Buddhist doctrine confirmed as the state religion.

Chinese Buddhism at this time was highly influenced by the Confucian doctrine of the state. To this end, the king was held in high regard, closely linked to the Buddha himself. Evidence of this connection is the *Inwang Kyong*, the Korean Buddhist sutra that paid homage to the king, and the *Paekchwa Kanghoe*, the ceremony in which all the monks of a monastery would congregate and pray for blessing for the state.

HWA RANG

During the sixth century the three kingdoms continued to draw sharp ideological lines between themselves and the expansionistic Chinese T'ang

Dynasty (618–907 C.E.). This movement toward war was based on the ongoing development of the individual societies and their continued invasions into one another's territories. This eventually led to an extended period of war between the three kingdoms and periodic conflicts with the T'ang to the north; this gave birth to the Hwa Rang warriors.

The Hwa Rang (Flowering Youth) warriors were first presented to the court of King Chin-hung in Silla in 576 C.E. King Chin-hung was the nephew of King Pop-hung, who had first introduced Buddhism into Silla.

Won Hwa (Original Flower) were the female leaders of the Hwa Rang. The term Won Hwa is often mistakenly used to represent a single individual; in fact, Won Hwa was a group of highly revered Buddhist nuns who spiritually guided these Buddhist monastic warriors. The Won Hwa formed a holy army, inspired by the Buddhist doctrine of no-self. They believed that their human forms were only portals through which, with proper action, they could raise their consciousnesses on to a higher level of Buddha-self. Thus, these warriors devoted their entire lives and all of their actions to their spiritual teacher, Won Hwa, who led them on the path of Buddhist warrior practices.

The first Hwa Rang were chosen in infancy, from the periphery of the kingdom, to be entered into the intensive training. At that time, this was a very high honor to bestow upon a child, as they were believed to be training to spend their lives in direct service to the Buddha. Once chosen, the children studied the *Nei Ching* and were schooled in the doctrines of Buddhism and martial warfare. By the time they reached late adolescence, not only were they proficient healers but they had also spent many years in meditation. Because of their training in these disciplines, they were able to lift their bodies and minds to levels of development not yet previously explored.

Hwa Rang warriors were all male; however, women participated in non-combat positions. Each division of Hwa Rang was led by a Won Hwa, who motivated and nurtured the young men as a matriarch.

The Hwa Rang were the first organized group to take the understanding of ki that is documented in the *Nei Ching,* join it with Buddhist meditation, and perform what were considered to be supernatural feats. Due to their ability to channel their ki energy at will and their discipline of non-attachment to the physical body, they could, for example, jump into the fierce current of the freezing Naklong River in winter without harm, and sit in deep meditation in the snows of the Taebaek Sanmaek Mountains where they were trained, clothed only in a loin cloth, and emerge unscathed.

When the first group of Hwa Rang were introduced to King Chin-hung, and their expertise revealed, he became certain that these warriors were the means by which he could defeat his attacking neighbors from the Korean Peninsula. Over years of war, King Chin-hung's soldiers had proven loyal to the kingdom but not exceptional in battle, as they were unable to defeat Koguryo and Paekche and the invasive T'ang Chinese. After seeing the Hwa Rang, King Chin-hung set about to organize a group of talented young noblemen who were exceedingly loyal to the throne and could be extensively trained in spiritual martial warfare by Won Hwa, with the hopes of using them as a secret weapon against his enemies.

As wealth and aristocracy were prevalent in Silla's royal court, King Chin-hung had difficulty finding willing participants to enter the strict order of the Hwa Rang. He enlisted the help of two beautiful court women to gather men around them and lure them into the Hwa Rang induction program.

These two women, Nam-mo and Chun-jung, were succesful in attracting several hundred young noblemen. Eventually, however, Chun-jung became jealous of Nam-mo, and she poisoned her wine and threw her, drugged, into the river, killing her. Chun-jung was subsequently put to death by the Silla royal court and the group of men surrounding them disbanded.

The next method the king used to induct young men into the Hwa Rang was to choose handsome young nobles, some as young as twelve years old, enticed by the honor of defending their kingdom. They were dressed in fine clothing and their faces painted with elaborate make-up. These boys were instructed in Buddhism, medical science according to the *Nei Ching,* poetry, and song. It was believed that those who fared well in these activities had the grace to become advanced warriors; thus, some of them were recommended to the Hwa Rang.

The second generation of Hwa Rang were trained in all forms of known warfare. They were taught the advanced practices of meditation, and that each of their physical movements was a service to their leader and an action ultimately in the service of the Buddha.

It was the belief of the Hwa Rang

that meditation could be practiced in the traditional sitting posture, and also when one focused one's personal spirit and entered into battle with a highly refined purpose and vision of a victorious outcome. Thus, the battles the Hwa Rang fought became spiritual exercises. To the youthful members of the Hwa Rang, the necessary killing of an opponent was beneficial for the ultimate karma of society. From the necessary mortal action they took, the Hwa Rang believed that they would gain good karma and be raised to a higher level of incarnation in their next birth.

It should be understood that during this period in Asian history there were numerous societies of Buddhist monks and nuns who retreated from the world and practiced not killing any form of life for any reason. This is what set the Hwa Rang apart from other Buddhist monastic groups. They were taught that the kingdom of Silla was the land of Maiterya (the future Buddha) and, as Silla warriors, killing for their society was a holy act. Furthermore, as Silla was the land of Maiterya, those of the Hwa Rang were believed to be incarnations of the Buddha. Therefore, the Hwa Rang believed that each life they took, in necessary combat, was a movement of meditation and would lead them to buddhahood.

The Hwa Rang were experts with the sword and the bow and masters of hand-to-hand combat. The Korean martial arts system of *Su Bak*—although Korean legend dates its inception to the time of the mythological Korean ruler King Tan-gun (2333 B.C.E.)—was the fighting system designed and developed by the Hwa Rang. Su Bak was a fierce hand-to-hand method of combat, a deadly art form designed to kill an opponent with one powerful strike.

Not only did the Hwa Rang use weapons and hand-to-hand combat, but they were the first warriors to perfect the technique of striking to *kup sul*, disabling vital pressure points to disrupt the opponent's flow of ki. Thus they were also the first warriors to use their understading of ki as a method of warfare.

The Korean martial art of Yu Sul was also developed at this time by the Hwa Rang. This martial art form was a softer grappling system of defense, utilizing ki energy as opposed to brute force. With cultural transmission between the island nation of Japan and the three Korean kingdoms taking place during this period, it is believed that Yu Sul was the predecessor to Japanese *Kenjutsu*, the forefather of Jujitsu.

The Hwa Rang were guided by a code of ethics laid down by the eminent monk Wong-wang.

1. Serve the king with loyalty.
2. Be obedient to your superiors.
3. Be honorable to all humankind.
4. Never retreat in battle.
5. Kill justly.

Once a Hwa Rang member was fully trained, he was put in command of a military troop composed of several hundred common soldiers. From the battles won by the Hwa Rang came the unification of Korea. However, this unification was achieved by very bloody means and many people of the Korean Peninsula were killed.

The ideology of Buddhist warriors was not unique to the kingdom of Silla and the Hwa Rang. Each of the three kingdoms on the Korean Peninsula possessed its group of young aristocratic holy warriors. In Koguryo, for example, existed the *Kyongdang* warriors. These were young men, generally in their teens, like the Hwa Rang, who practiced strict Buddhist doctrine, lived a celibate life, and strived to cultivate high moral virtue. Documentation of the youthful warriors of the other two Korean kindgoms is not as complete as that of the Hwa Rang. This is in no

small part due to the fact that the warriors from these states were defeated and, thus, much of their history was lost or destroyed.

After the unification of Korea and the defeat of the invasive Chinese T'ang Dynasty, the focus of the Korean peoples rapidly began to shift away from confrontation toward more philosophical objectives. The need for Hwa Rang warriors declined, and they began to disband. For a time, due to their refined knowledge, understanding of ki, and healing abilities, they remained a group specializing in Buddhist philosophy, healing, music, and poetry. They became known for their *hyang-ga* (native songs), gentle, rhythmic, poetic songs. These songs, written by Hwa Rang or Buddhist monks, were believed to be vehicles for healing and connecting with the energy of the universe. The early Buddhism of Korea held tightly to its reverence for intervention from the ever-present spirit world, so the music of the Hwa Rang was performed for the purpose of worldly and karmic healing. The Hwa Rang survived until the end of the seventh century, after which there is no evidence of their existence.

The Korean martial arts system Su Bak became known as *Tae Kyon* during the seventh century. Tae Kyon, written in the Chinese characters, meant "Push Shoulder" and the art continued to be practiced by the Korean military. The Korean military text *Moo Yea Do Bok Tong Ki*, written in the fifteenth century, details the prescribed practices of the advanced warrior based on the disciplines developed by the Hwa Rang. This text, in association with the ongoing refinements to martial techniques, has defined the Korean warrior until the modern era.

JAPAN

From the Korean kingdom of Paekche, Chinese influence first reached Japan at the bequest of King Kunch-ogo (346–375 C.E.). Two Korean scholars, A-Chikki and Wang-In, were sent to Japan to instruct the Japanese crown prince in the Confucian doctrines. They brought with them ten copies of the *Analects of Confucius* and one copy of the *Chien Cha Wen* (*The Thousand Character Classic*). This first transmission of Confucian thought is one of the most culturally influential events in the history of ancient Japan.

This first cultural transmission from Korea and later interaction with China had a great impact on the island nation of Japan; from this time in Japanese history great tombs, previously never established in Japan, are inscribed with depictions of mainland Asian warriors. In addition, armor and weapons made from an advanced metallurgy that Japan did not previously possess came to be used.

With the introduction of new methods of statesmanship and warfare, a group of rulers emerged from the Yamato plain in the southern region of the main Japanese island, Honshu. Their exploits are detailed in the first written chronicle of Japanese history titled *Kojiki* (*The Record of Ancient Matters*), authored in approximately 712 C.E. These military rulers were highly influenced by the ideals of Confucian-based Chinese and Korean statesmanship. With superior weaponry and military tactics, they began to take control of the country by first overpowering then forming alliances with tribal chieftains. As time progressed and their political hold tightened, they began to integrate Confucian ideology into the indigenous Japanese religion of Shintoism. These rulers believed that they were chosen by the sun goddess to govern the country; they placed the sun goddess at the pinnacle of worship in Shintoism, thus assuring that they too would be worshipped as descendants of the gods. By the end of the fourth century they had achieved political unity over the island nation of Japan and set the stage for the later samurai class of military rulers to emerge.

Again from the Korean state of Paekche, Buddhist monks were sent to Japan in the sixth century, introducing Buddhism to the island nation. The Buddhist monk Kwall-uk (Kanroku in Japanese) crossed the Sea of Japan in 602 C.E., bringing with him a large number of Buddhist sutras, historical books, medical books, and works on astronomy, geography, and the occult arts. Kwall-uk was instrumental in the founding of the Sanron school of Buddhism in Japan. As there is no evidence of Chinese medical practices in Japan before this point, it is believed that this is when the knowledge of ki, detailed in the *Nei Ching,* was first transmitted from Korea to Japan. After Kwall-uk's arrival Chinese and Korean medicine expanded rapidly throughout Japan.

In 607 C.E. Crown Prince Shotoku set about the task of integrating Buddhism with Japan's native Shinto religion. His belief was that the Japanese gods were manifestations of the Buddha and, as such, should receive the same reverence as the Buddha. Shotoku sent political envoys to Korea and China to gain deeper understanding of Buddhist thought. It took many

years for him to convince the royal hierarchy of the importance of Buddhism, and for the Japanese peoples to accept a new god into their already established religious belief system.

The first Buddhist temple, Horyu-ji, was founded in 607 in Nara, Japan, due to the efforts of Prince Shotoku. Japanese Buddhist temples became the center of vast land holdings. The Todai-ji Temple was established in 758, holding possession of over five thousand houses from which the temple's abbot collected rent and taxes. In 968 two priests trained in warfare, one from the Todai-ji Temple and the other from the Kofuku-ji Temple, actually entered into battle with one another over a dispute of land ownership. The Buddhism embraced in Japan was not solely a means for enlightenment, which it was later to become, but instead was a wealthy institution, prone to internal conflicts.

By the end of the tenth century warrior Buddhist monks were known as *sohei.* These monks were generally peasants and petty criminals who were recruited by the temples as a means to expand a temple's army and defend against attacks instigated by other temples and landholders. These warrior monks were given living quarters and food and were trained in the martial practices in exchange for their defense of the temple and its holdings.

The sohei of the various temples formed groups of warriors that were feared by other military factions in Japan. Each temple formulated its own school of fighting, which led to the development of many new martial art systems in Japan. The mind-set of the sohei was in sharp contrast to that of the Korean Hwa Rang. The Hwa Rang were soldier monks devoted to enlightenment, whereas the sohei were refined warriors and not very religious monks.

It was the Japanese *gakusho*, the scholar priests—monks who were on the high end of the temple hierarchy and could generally trace their lineage to the royal family—who not only gained the spoils of the Japanese Buddhist expansionism but who also set the stage for the evolution of Buddhism into the enlightened philosophy that it has become.

The gakusho were similar in structure and social placement to that of the Catholic Church's upper level hierarchy during this same period of world history. The prevailing difference between the gakusho and that of the Catholic Church was that there was no central location, like Rome, and no ruling figure head, like the Pope, to guide all of the Buddhist temples across Japan.

The gakusho possessed no overriding governing body. Instead, the gakusho of each individual temple or sect dictated their own rules and elevated their own leaders. This allowed the various schools of Buddhism to evolve in Japan. These schools were generally bound more by geographical determinates than by philosophic or religious idealism. Ultimately, many of these sects fell into decline, leaving only a few that flourished.

The gakusho not only set the standard for Buddhist study in medieval Japan, but they also controlled the wealth and land holdings of each individual temple or Buddhist sect. Although the gakusho claimed poverty, in following traditional Buddhist vows, they, nonetheless, wielded enormous political power and lived an embellished life.

SAMURAI

By the eighth century the samurai emerged as an entity in Japan. The first samurai were military retainers who, for the most part, were illiterate rural tenant farmers who farmed between battles. The word *samurai* is based on the Japanese verb *samurau*, which means to serve. Thus, the word *samurai* connotes service to one's overlord.

The early samurai were not always willing participants in battle. They were often taken from their farms and forced to defend the property they found themselves living on as tenants. Eventually the samurai came to be elite militarists, leaving their fields behind, with an independent moral culture that separated them from the rest of Japanese society.

Samurai Shogunate

The title *bushi* (warrior) was given to samurai who formed clans to defend themselves against the various warring factions, especially in northern Japan. By the beginning of the twelfth century, the original rulers of Japan, each claiming descent from the sun goddess, separated into different, well-established, powerful warrior families. They began to battle against the controlling nobility and other large *buke* (clans) that were struggling for power. From these wars emerged three ruling families: the Fujiwara, who controlled the government; the Taira; and the Minamoto—all believing themselves to be the rightful divine rulers of Japan.

The Fujiwara were the first to be overthrown, by the Taira. Then, in the Gempei War (1180–1185), the Taira family was displaced by the Minamoto clan. Minamoto no Yoritomo (1147–1199) established the first samurai-based military government (samurai shogunate), which, by establishing the Kamakura Shogunate, led Japan into the Kamakura period (1192–1333)—a period when samurai aristocrats governed the country with military rule.

The Takeda Family

The eldest son of Minamoto no Yoritomo, Yoshikiyo, moved away from the central clan to the area in the north known as Kai. There he founded a new branch of the Minamoto clan, known as Kaigengitakeda: *kai* from the region; *gengi,* the original Chinese root of their family name; and *takeda,* the new chosen family name. That is how the famous Takeda family originated.

The Takeda family had many powerful members who influenced the growth of refined warfare on the island of Japan. Takeda Nobumitsu (1162–1248) reorganized the entire Minamoto system of martial arts, renaming it *Genji no Heiho.** Takeda Shingen (1521–1573)

* During this period of Japanese history, language was written with Chinese characters. Because Chinese writing is symbolic and not based on phonetic language, the characters are open to interpretation and change.

was the author of the *Shingen Hatto,* which became the code of provincial law for samurai-ruled Japan.

Through its continued extensive interaction with learned Buddhist monks, the Takeda family was instrumental in the advancement of the understanding of ki. Takeda Sokaku (Minamoto no Masayoshi, 1858–1943) was born into a family of Shinto priests in the Aizu region of Japan. In early childhood he began to study the sword at the Ono Itto-ryu school. During this period the samurai were still allowed to roam without restrictions. He then entered the life of a wandering *ronin,* an independant samurai warrior who traveled freely to work as a guard or assassin for wealthy landowners and politicians. He was a fierce warrior, killing all of his opponents.

Eventually, Japanese rulers began to curtail the exploits of the outdated ronin. Takeda Sokaku opened a school of martial arts, naming the system he taught Daito Ryu Aikijitsu (the school of the large sword meeting with ki). At his *dojo* (school) he trained the likes of the founder of Aikido, Ueshiba Morihei, and the father of Korean Hapkido, Choi Yong Shul (whose Japanese name was Yoshida Asao). Aikido and Hapkido are the two modern martial arts systems that have been funda-

mental to the propagation of ki-oriented self-defense.

THE FORMATION OF ZEN

After the Gempei War, Japan produced new Buddhist sects that contributed to the refinement of Buddhist understanding throughout the world. The first of these sects was founded by Honen-Shonim (born in 1133), a monk who was disheartened by the militaristic, competitive nature of Buddhism in Japan. He founded the Jodo, or Pure Land, sect of Buddhism in Japan. The basic precept of the Jodo school was that the world was inherently evil, and so the attainment of enlightenment was impossible within it. Therefore, the faithful who had lived a holy life could only experience enlightenment at the moment of their death.

An off-shoot of Jodo, known as Shinshu, was founded by Shinran Shonin in 1224. He taught that if one were to continually repeat the names of the Buddha, one could, in fact, reach enlightenment during one's lifetime. He also rejected vegetarianism, which was practiced by other Japanese Buddhists, as well as the practice of celibacy.

Although these new schools of

Buddhism attracted numerous followers, the samurai, as a whole, did not join them. In 1192 the metaphysical Ch'an school of Buddhism was reintroduced into Japan from China after its failure three hundred years earlier. It was brought by a monk named Eisai (1141–1215), who belonged to the Chinese Buddhist school of Huanglong. Eisai formed the *Rinzai-shu,* or Rinzai sect, of Buddhism, and Ch'an became known as Zen. Zen Buddhism emphasized the need for meditation, claiming that *satori* (enlightenment) came from within as opposed to being the result of prayer or divine grace. The samurai class readily embraced this system of thought, as it allowed them to remain independent.

The teachings of the Zen master Dogen (1200–1253), who founded the Soto school of Zen Buddhism, were fundamental to the practices of meditation that were developed by Japanese Buddhists and samurai. When Ch'an was reintroduced to Japan from China, it brought with it the continued debate over the best method of meditation. There was the *Kung-an* school of thought, which emphasized a gradual clearing of the mind; and the *Mo-cha* understanding, which spoke of sudden enlightenment. Dogen believed that *zazen* (sitting meditation) was the true

root of Buddhism and the path to enlightenment, which could occur at any instance, once an individual's mind was settled and ready to embody Buddha-mind. Meditation was strongly emphasized over ritual religious practices and intellectual analysis.

Zen embraces emptiness. It does not focus upon results gained from physical actions. There is no project, no occupation, no dwelling in past, present, or future. This experience occurs suddenly and spontaneously in the meditator, as a state of complete awareness and relaxation, devoid of preconceptions. This mode of understanding may be hard for the Western mind to grasp due to the fact that Zen philosophy is based in paradox: action within nonaction, movement within nonmovement.

As Zen matured in Japan, the samurai helped to expand the focus of zazen to additional realms that brought physical movement into an expression of meditation. The gakusho priests took the meditative understandings of Zen and advanced them to embrace the methods of samurai warfare. *Iaido,* the meditation of drawing the sword was born, as was *Kyudo,* the meditative art of archery. From these redefined physical meditation techniques, the martial arts were advanced to a new level of spiritual understanding that is still in practice today.

For the samurai, the result of embracing Zen was the transcendence of technique altogether and the notion of abiding in nontechnique. With this understanding, they practiced the martial arts toward the attainment of satori. Therefore, in regard to the advanced techniques of warfare, it was the spiritual intention of the samurai to become one with the essence of their physical movements. The act of drawing a sword became a movement in meditation. The pulling back of the bow and the release of the arrow became a practice for clearing the mind and seeing one's enlightened nature. Through these metaphysical actions, the samurai dropped the focus on the self and embraced the emptiness of satori.

THE BIRTH OF BUSHIDO

The ideology that would much later give birth to the notion of *Bushido* (the way of the warrior) first emerged in Japan during the Yamato period (400–645 C.E.). This warrior ideology was an unwritten code of conduct followed by the samurai. This warrior's code firmly took hold in the later part of the Heian period (795–1185), during which time warrior ideology

evolved into a formal system of moral conduct. The code dictated that the true warrior kept his sword sheathed, avoided violence, and lived in peace with all beings—unless violence was absolutely necessary. The warrior's inner mastery of aggression shined outward, embracing all creatures.

As Japanese society evolved, the warrior's code was continually redefined. In the thirteenth century, *Kyuba no Michi* (The Way of the Bow and the Horse), came to be the formalized written credo of warrior conduct.

Yamaga Soke (1622–1685) was the first to formally combine the words *bushi* (warrior) and *do* (way). Then, in 1716, the first written code of the warrior to be authored since *Kyuba no Michi* emerged, titled *Hagakure* (Hidden Underneath the Leaves).

Hagakure

Hagakure was written by Yamamoto Tsunetomo, who had been in the service of Nabeshima Mitsushige, a *daimyo* (overlord) of the Saga prefecture, for most of his life. When Mitsushige died in 1700, Tsunetomo asked and was granted permission to retire from governmental service and become a Buddhist monk. He moved to a small hermitage in Kurotsuchibaru, Japan.

Tashiro Tsuramoto, a retired samurai, begin to visit Tsunetomo in 1710. The two became friends and enjoyed philosophical discussions about warfare and Japanese culture in general. From these discussions came *Hagakure* in 1716.

The dialogue that makes up *Hagakure* is representative of the two primary influences in Tsunetomo's life: Zen Buddhism and the Confucian doctrines of state. Tsunetomo had two influential teachers: Tannen (died 1680), a Zen Buddhist priest; and Ishida Ittei, a Confucian scholar. The blending of these two traditions is portrayed in *Hagakure*. The book is not written in a linear format, but rather, presents seemingly random stories, thoughts, and ideas quoted from various sources. Many of these tales were narrated in a tone that criticized Japanese religious and social mores of the time. Nonetheless, it was Tsunetomo's belief that the path of the samurai ultimately leads to death, and death was the greatest gift one could give one's master.

The Code of Bushido

In 1905 Nitobe Inazo (1862–1933) published the doctrine that came to be known as the code of Bushido.

1. Loyalty to the emperor is essential duty.
2. Respect your superiors; be considerate of your juniors.
3. Bravery in battle is to be honored.
4. Faith in the way leads to greatness.
5. Simple living is the path to enlightenment.

During this late period of Japanese history, Buddhism was prevalent, but a soldier's duty was more closely linked to the Confucian idea of loyalty to the state. At this time, expansionism was practiced by the Japanese as it was believed that the Japanese were the divine race, and thus, their conquest of other Asian nations was just and righteous. With that attitude in mind, this published code of Bushido can be seen as influenced by the government, designed to indoctrinate sodiers into focusing their loyalty on Japan.

OKINAWA

Japanese contact with the Ryukyu Islands, of which Okinawa is a part, began in 616 C.E., when approximately thirty Okinawans were escorted to Nara, Japan, to the court of Shotoku Taishi, to be educated in Japanese culture. From this point forward Japanese contact with and influence on the Ryukyu Islands intensified. Buddhism arrived rather haphazardly from Japan in the thirteenth century when Zenkan, a Japanese monk, was shipwrecked. He constructed a temple at the old capital of Urasoe and thus Buddhism was introduced to the islands. Although Buddhism was only marginally accepted initially, by the fifteenth century there were several Buddhist temples established on the Ryukyu Islands, predominately in the capital of Shuri.

The martial art of the Ryukyu Islands, known originally as *Okinawa-te*, can be traced to the seventh century. The Ryukyu Islands are in close proximity to China and cultural interactions took place. Chinese martial arts were first introduced in the islands through Chinese Taoist and Buddhist monks during the late seventh century.

One of the most historically influential contributions to the development of the Okinawan martial arts was the relocation of thirty-six Chinese families to Okinawa in 1392. Their tradition of *Kempo* (Chinese boxing) was absorbed by Okinawan culture and is the basis of Okinawa-te.

Throughout history Japan and China fought to overpower one an-

other. As the methods for transporting troops over long distances evolved, the Ryukyu Islands became an interim port for battle between the two nations. Because of the useful location of the Ryukyu Islands, they were understood to be of great strategic military importance. Although attempted conquest of the Ryukyu Islands continued throughout the centuries, it wasn't until 1609 that Japan succeeded in taking political control over the island nation.

Due to the ongoing attacks launched against Okinawa by invasive Japanese, in 1599 Sho Nei, the king of Okinawa, asked the Chinese emperor to send soldiers to help with defense—which was done. Through this contact, the Okinawa military force was formally schooled in Chinese Kempo and Chinese martial arts. In 1609, however, Okinawa lost its autonomy to Japan. During the cultural invasion that ensued, Okinawans banded together in small groups and avidly trained in developing their martial arts systems to protect their cultural identity. In this early period there were three distinct styles of Okinawan martial arts: *Naha-te*, *Shuri-te*, and *Tomari-te*.

By the eighteenth century the modern characteristics of Okinawan martial arts were solidified. The systems that were formalized—and are still taught today—were: *Shorin-ryu*, *Shore-ryu*, *Goju-ryu*, and *Uechi-ryu*. During this period, the Japanese martial arts were integrated with these Okinawan systems, and by the 1880s the term *Kara-te* came into common usage in Japan. This is the name accepted by Japan and later used worldwide to refer to the martial arts that were transmitted from China to Okinawa, and then on to Japan.

THE SAMURAI PATHWAY TO ENLIGHTENMENT

At the point in history when warfare became linked with Buddhism the stage was set for the martial arts to become a spiritual discipline. This was exemplified when Zen came to be practiced by the Japanese samurai. Although other religions have been practiced by martial artists, as many are today, it was the Zen Buddhism of Japan, practiced by samurai, which truly came to define the martial arts as a spiritual path.

Due to the cultural climate of Japan, Buddhism coexisted with the native Shinto religion and the accepted Confucian doctrines; Japanese politics, while influencing various aspects of Buddhism, did not hamper its practice and development. Government, however, did have control in other Asian nations where religion and culture were dominated by state ideology. As a result, Japan was the only Asian nation, from the twelfth century onward, in which the path of the spiritual warrior was allowed to unfold without government intrusion.

Starting with the middle of the twelfth century, practitioners of Japanese martial arts immersed themselves in the quest for enlightenment through the techniques of warfare. The expression *seishi o choetsu* refers to the way the highly trained warrior transcends thoughts of life and death that arise especially in war. He achieves this by understanding that physical life is temporal, whereas spiritual life is forever. To sharpen their minds to the point at which fear of death did not dominate their actions in combat, the samurai practiced a regime of zazen and physical meditation techniques taught by masters of their weapons. The philosophy of Zen Buddhism was at the center of all of the samurai's meditations.

One-Pointedness

The Zen teachers of classic *Budo* (the way of combat) taught the samurai that to raise themselves to a higher level of consciousness they needed to focus with their entire physical and spiritual being. From this one-pointedness of body, mind, and spirit, one could not only become a superior warrior, but would ultimately experience satori (enlightenment) through one's actions.

Attaining the precisely focused one-pointedness of body, mind, and spirit is known by the Japanese word *tomaru*, which, literally translated, means "abiding." The main hindrance to the achievement of *tomaru* is *bonno*, which means "disturbed feeling." Bonno witnesses the bushi losing his calm meditative mind, which makes him vulnerable in combat.

In the mind of the spiritual warrior, inner peace should never be lost. If it becomes lost, then the mind is distracted and can be controlled by fear, desire, and ego gratification. If the warrior falls prey to these emotions he is easily defeated in battle by the bushi who is steadfast in his clarity.

There are two perceptions of consciousness in Japanese meditative understanding that came to define the bushi: the first is *kon* and the second is *haku*. Kon refers to the conscious or higher soul and haku is the lower or material soul. The bushi who is a slave to his ego is driven by haku; the bushi who has divine purpose is led by kon.

The spiritual warrior is trained to focus his mind on the higher consciousness and never let it be distracted by emotional or material stimulation. This is accomplished through meditation techniques that train the warrior to always put compassion before his own emotions.

The first level of meditation is formal, seated zazen. From extensive periods of seated meditation, during which the mind is acutely focused, the first level of spiritual clarity, or *makoto*, is achieved. Makoto means emptied, or stainless, mind. The warrior who has refined his mind to this level encounters *prajna*. Prajna is the universal, immovable wisdom available to all beings: immovable, not in the sense of becoming stagnant, but firm and steady in one-pointed wisdom.

Prajna is evident in the spiritual warrior when he has let go of his individual ego. Ego is shed by coming to understand that one's physical actions are transient and lead to nothing more than an insignificant movement in the physical world. One's spiritual actions, however, lead to satori. Satori can be reached instantaneously; one can achieve enlightenment at any moment. Only the belief that one is not already enlightened prevents one from reaching satori.

Prajna is not a thought. Prajna is

the immediacy of mastered action. If a warrior has to contemplate his actions in a battle, then he is lost in the realms of the thinking mind and will be defeated.

It must be understood that the essence of Budo is based in the Zen meditative understanding of no-thought. The Japanese expression for this is *mushin*, which translates as "no-mind," or more precisely "original mind." No-mind is the state in which the warrior abides—not lost in the battle or fixated on the mundane experiences of everyday life.

Temporal fixation is known as *ushin*, which leads the mind from one fixation to the next. With this mind-set as a basis, no-mind is impossible. Therefore, the bushi consciously leaves behind the world of thinking and ego-fixation by refining his mind through the practice of Zen meditation.

With the mind abiding in mushin, the warrior is free to reflect the world as if he were a mirror. In this state of mind, the bushi is at harmony with his surroundings and does not desire things to be any different than the way they are. In battle, he is free to react appropriately because he is not burdened by any prescribed response to a specific assault. Thus, his physical actions are based in the Zen understanding of no-action. Action within no-action is the key for the spiritual warrior.

2
THE MIND
OF THE
SPIRITUAL WARRIOR

The central point of the spiritual warrior's training is psychological control. Without control over the emotions a martial artist is easily swayed by momentary desires and from those are born egotism and a disregard for the principles of universal peace.

A martial artist can never truly move to higher realms of consciousness if he is not in control of the psychological factors that affect his life. Therefore, the first area of study that the modern martial artist undertakes on the path to enlightenment is that of mindfulness toward himself, the world around him,

and the universe as a whole.

Shugyo is a Japanese term that means "spiritual polishing." In English, shugyo would be more easily understood as "spiritual training." The process of conscious mental refinement is what sets the spiritual warrior apart from the common martial artist, who focuses only on the development of physical techniques. The spiritual warrior, however, embraces *banyu aigo*, universal love and compassion for all living things.

The spiritual warrior trains his body and mind with the intention of making himself a positive vehicle for universal consciousness and of aiding all of those in need around him. To effect this positive conveyance of energy, the spiritual warrior holds a clear understanding of how he as an individual most effectively interacts with other people and nature. With this understanding, battles are won without ever being fought and goodness prevails.

Honor

Honor is at the heart of every activity the spiritual warrior undertakes. Honor is never based in self-righteousness. Honor is developing one's own self-worth in perspective with the grand scheme of the universe. An honorable deed is doing something that needs to be done, one that is accomplished either for the good of humankind, the good of a singular individual, or simply because it is necessary. An honorable deed is one that does not require compensation, either financial or emotional.

Anything in life can be done honorably. The difference between an honorable deed and a dishonorable deed is determined solely by the individual. A dishonorable action occurs when the actor acts with a self-gratifying motivation. An honorable man never takes more than he is due. He never takes from those who cannot give. He never practices deception while accomplishing his actions. He doesn't allow desire or his ego to motivate the actions he takes. Many people justify their actions by believing their gain, be it economic, emotional, or physical gratification, is worth what it costs others. Justification is never the path of honor for the spiritual warrior. The spiritual warrior would rather suffer himself, gaining insightful wisdom, than cause another person to suffer in any way.

Morality

Honor gives birth to morality. Morals are not the ideology of a specific culture in a specific period of time but are based on universal right and wrong. Right is always right, wrong is always wrong. If you must think about your actions to justify them, they are not morally right.

The entire world appreciates and embraces right actions. The entire world looks down on those actions that are wrong.

Truthfulness

Truthfulness is honesty with yourself and with those around you. There is never a reason to deceive another person, intentionally or unintentionally. Deception is dishonorable.

Respect for All Living Beings

The spiritual warrior understands that all creatures—humans and others—have a purpose in the world. As all have a purpose, all beings must be respected. From mutual respect, divine understanding is born.

Those who do not respect others are lost in the falsehood that they possess a superiority over other people and other creatures. Without a weapon could a martial artist defeat a tiger? No. Thus, who is superior? What happens when the supposedly superior individual needs to enlist the help of a person he believes below himself? The person who is needed, no doubt, possesses skills the "superior" person does not have. At that moment, who is superior?

To grow spiritually, the warrior must understand that each entity on this planet has a purpose to serve. Although you may not appreciate the function of every being, you must, nonetheless, respect the fact that they have a purpose or they would not be here. For example, take the case of someone whose lifestyle you disapprove of or don't appreciate. This is not to say you must associate with them, there is no reason to disturb your peace by associating with someone you do not like or someone who could get you into unnecessary confrontations; however, as a spiritual warrior you are enlightened enough to know that that person, too, serves a divine purpose.

Divine Perfection

Divine perfection is the understanding that everything in this world happens for a reason. Everything from the most exciting event to the worst catastrophe happens in accordance with a divine purpose. This understanding is expressed in Japanese as *takelbu*, which means "divine truth, goodness, and beauty," or "universal righteousness."

There are times that we human beings do not have the power or the understanding to see an event in its entirety. As time passes, however, the enlightened individual witnesses how what appeared to be a very negative experience at one point gives way to a positive experience in a later time. Without seemingly negative events in our life, we may not have been forced to move forward to learning and gaining what we did at a later time. Accepting divine perfection allows you to witness that all events in this world occur for a divine purpose.

For an example the martial artist can relate to, say you lose a sparring match. Are you going to stop training, believing you are a horrible fighter, and never spar again? No, what you will do is learn from your mistakes and move forward, train harder, and the next time emerge victorious.

This style of learning, from losing, is fundamental to the mind of the martial artist. In life, there will be loss. What is loss? The undesired outcome of a specific event.

If you desired to enter a fighting match and lose, would your losing be a defeat? If you no longer liked an object, would its being taken from you be a theft?

Look deeply into your mind and see what you truly desire.

Loss and gain are all based on individual desires. They are temporal in nature because new desires will come with life experience.

Take the loss, take the injury, take the dishonor, and view them from all sides dispassionately. What can you learn? How can your life be positively affected by your endurance? Although you don't like the outcome, grow from it. Move on.

View any negative experience as a divine pathway to becoming a more enlightened being.

As a spiritual warrior you accept the rightness of the universe. By accepting rightness you experience a free mind, unbound by desires for different outcomes than actually occurred. From this experience you can maintain a state of meditative equanimity because your emotions are not unnecessarily stirred.

Take action, but do not become bound by your action. Experience the results, but do not get lost in the outcome.

Intuition

By accepting divine perfection the spiritual warrior begins to develop insightful understanding of what lays ahead. Some people may refer to this as psychic ability or intuition, but in fact, it is simply a result of the process of learning not to be swayed by specific desired outcomes.

If you don't care if you win or lose, you will not be unduly affected by joy or anger. Thus, you will not be unduly motivated to achieve a desired result. From equanimity, harmony with the universe is developed, and from harmony with the universe comes an innate sense of what is to come.

Accepting divine perfection allows you to be free.

Confrontation

A person who is not keenly in control of his emotions can be easily lured into unnecessary confrontations, both physical and emotional. What is an unnecessary confrontation? Any battle that is not waged for the sole purpose of maintaining universal rightness.

By allowing yourself to be lured into an unnecessary confrontation, you give the provoker power over you. This is seen quite easily when you observe a person who is attempting to drag you into some kind of altercation. Before the fight begins, you will witness a sense of power and happiness emanating from your provoker. This is because in his mind he has already begun to take control over you, thus winning the fight.

Most people feel this sense of power on a subconscious level, and they do not even realize that they are receiving psychological stimulation from the act of provoking, so they continue to encounter people in this fashion.

The confrontational mentality is the reason most provokers win the battles they instigate, thus assuring themselves of justification for what they are doing. As instigators, they are mentally prepared before the battle ever begins. The individual who is accosted is gen-erally not in mental readiness for a fight, so he is easily overpowered.

It has long been a martial arts teaching that a warrior should be prepared for battle at any time. This way of thinking keeps the individual constantly on edge, however. Peace of mind is not achieved this way. As energy always attracts similar energy, the martial artist who is constantly in wait for the upcoming battle will discover that he, in fact, will always encounter hostile situations.

The spiritual warrior's body and mind are prepared for battle at any time. Her thoughts do not dwell on potential battles, however. The spiritual warrior's mind abides in peace. If a confrontation comes, it comes, but it is allowed to enter on its own path of divine perfection; it is not expected.

The Zen samurai Takuan (1573–1645) developed the principle of *mutekatsu*. According to mutekatsu, it is possible to defeat an enemy without ever raising a hand or lifting a weapon. Mutekatsu teaches that one should avoid conflict by all possible means. This is accomplished by not allowing your opponent to make an attack. In the modern world, we understand this teaching to mean that we should not run from altercations, but neither should we place ourselves in situations where confrontation is imminent.

Mutekatsu teaches that if confrontation is unavoidable, then the way to defeat the opponent is to not engage him at all, but instead, to allow him to become exhausted by your anticipation and deflection of his attacks.

By allowing someone to anger you with words or meaningless actions, you give them power over your emotions and thus, your inner peace. If you are lured into a senseless verbal or physical exchange, the outcome can never be worthy of your energy, even if you emerge victorious, for you will not have waged an honorable fight. Instead, you will have simply lowered yourself by engaging in a battle of egos. In a battle of egos there is never a rightful victor.

When someone entices someone else into purposeless warfare it is because of desire: desire to appear more powerful, more skilled, more intelligent; or in the case of the socially insecure, the desire to be able to disrupt the peace of another. For all of these reasons, the spiritual warrior never allows herself to be seduced into battle. In the same way, the spiritual warrior never pursues unnecessary battle, whether in the form of physical confrontations, emotional arguments, struggling to gain power in a group, or simply jockeying for position in a traffic jam.

Pursuit of violence always ends in destruction.

How do you feel when you have unnecessarily placed yourself in confrontation with another individual? Is there ever any lasting enlightenment?

You may win a battle, but you will have gained nothing if the battle was fought for no reason.

Surrender and be like the wind, forceful without ever being seen.

Physical Battle

There are three things the spiritual warrior must assess before entering into a physical altercation:

1. Are you angered? If so, why?
2. Will your potential victory in a confrontation right a wrong?
3. Will your potential victory benefit others?

Anger

If you are angry when you enter a fight, your mind is not free. It is burdened with emotional obstacles to victory.

An angry warrior is never a conscious warrior.

Anger is an emotion. Emotions come and go. Emotions rarely last for more than a few moments. For this reason anger is never a reason to enter into a physical battle.

Anger is an addictive emotion. It is addictive because it causes the body's adrenal glands to release hormones and the blood pressure to rise, thus, causing stimulation. The mind of someone addicted to anger subconsciously finds reasons to produce this emotion.

Anger is never a positive emotion. It may stimulate you, it may even motivate you to enact change, but its continued experience causes much disharmony to your body.

The question to ask yourself before you enter into an anger-induced fight is, why am I angry? Generally, the answer is, "I have been wronged and my anger was provoked." Although this may well be the case, you must hold the broader view to truly walk the path of the spiritual warrior.

How were you wronged? Was it a physical action, such as a push, a shove, or your car being cut off in traffic? Was it a verbal insult, or the insulting of someone you know? In any of these cases, the actions that were taken were fleeting in nature, and, in fact, quite meaningless in the overall scheme of the universe.

Generally, the type of person who commonly instigates and participates in meaningless battles is one who is emotionally insecure, although he may appear to be physically well developed. This is one of the primary problems with modern, commercial martial arts schools; they take virtually anyone into their classes and train them. In many martial arts schools the only criteria for joining is the individual's desire to learn how to fight more competently. Many emotionally unstable and insecure people have been trained in fighting competently. Instead of focusing on the inner development the martial arts teach, such a person simply allows his insecurities to become exaggerated. In this way, many an evil adversary has been unleashed on society by martial arts instructors.

In times past, when a student wished to train in the martial arts, he was first expected to go through a long period of apprenticeship before actually being taught in the martial ways; those who did not possess the right frame of mind rarely could complete the induction process of cleaning the dojo and helping the instructor and his advanced students. This method of dojo acceptance by its very nature selected a certain caliber of individual.

In modern times, many unsuitable candidates have entered the martial arts and have received training in advanced forms of physical combat.

Many of them possess a devil-may-care attitude toward physical altercations. If you look deeply into the eyes of these martial practitioners, you see that they have no fear because they have nothing to lose. Certainly the psychological, emotional, and economic circumstances that made this person who he is can be partially blamed for his condition. Nonetheless, he is the most dangerous type of person with whom to enter into angered combat, because his psychological, and oftentimes physical, conditioning give him the overall edge in angered battle. The only way this kind of person should be encountered physically is with a clear mind, not bound by anger. With a clear mind and years of martial training you will be the one with the winning edge.

In a forced physical confrontation, it is very difficult for anyone to separate the emotions of the moment from the larger-scale picture of what is important in the universe. Ask yourself these questions before ever entering a fight:

1. Will my winning this physical confrontation make me a better person?
2. Will my winning make the person I defeat a more enlightened individual?

As all answers to philosophic questions are subjective, the mind-set of the individual asking them will play a great role in how they are answered. Nonetheless, by developing the ability, through spiritual practice, to step back from the emotions of the moment and look at the "big picture," you will come to the appropriate conclusion, giving rise to the universal good.

Competition

One of the key problems with many modern martial arts systems is that they breed competition. In fact, many martial arts systems are based solely on physical competition. Through staged altercations the practitioners may well become more competent combatants, but they will, no doubt, develop a less-than-spiritual understanding of their art.

Competition is the lowest level of martial understanding. Competition causes the martial artist to become unnaturally stimulated for little or no reason. It causes the adrenal glands to produce large amounts of hormones, which cause the heart rate to accelerate, the blood pressure to rise, and various other uncomfortable symptoms to occur. In competitive situations, the physical body is set out of balance, and peace cannot be embraced.

On the subject of physical confrontations, there is always one fact that remains true: there will always be someone who is a better fighter than you are. Although you may not have encountered that person yet, if you continue to enter competitions it is certain that you will. This is the nature of human existence.

When you are young, you are naturally quick, strong, and you have lasting endurance. As age comes upon you, your reflexes slow down and your bones and muscles weaken. The long-trained martial artist, hopefully, develops insightful wisdom with his years, to overcome his declining physical condition.

The spiritual warrior never enters a competitive battle. Why? Because he never seeks the gratification that comes from victory in these types of altercations.

In physical combat the spiritual warrior possesses the ability to defeat even the strongest of emotionally motivated adversaries. Such a victory, however, is never based on the competitive spirit; it is based on understanding of the universal ways of life and the movement of energy.

Defeat and Victory

In life there are endless confrontations for those who engage in competition. Victory and defeat are not limited to the ring, the mat, or the streets. The spiritual warrior defines a victory or a defeat according to how it deepens his understanding of human communication.

If someone sneaks up on you from behind and hits you over the head with a club, knocking you out before you have the chance to react and defend yourself, is that defeat? No, it is not—although some practitioners of martial arts may falsely believe that all trained martial artists should be able to sense oncoming danger before they actually encounter it. This type of power is only found in legends. As human beings we are limited by the factors that make up the human form and, although we may strive to train our bodies and minds to be stronger or better than the average person's, we are still human.

You cannot defeat what you cannot see coming.

With this understanding as a basis, we know that at times of face-to-face physical confrontation, techniques may be launched at us that we do not see coming or do not have time or the ability to react against. Is being taken by surprise a defeat? No, at that moment, you simply did not possess the ability to effectively deal with the offensive technique in the appropriate defensive manner.

Say you enter a second match with the same opponent. He unleashes the same offensive technique at you that he used the last time. The strike makes contact with you. Is that defeat? Yes, it is. Defeat is when the martial artist believes that he already knows how to win in any physical altercation and he gives up his continuous vigilance in refining his fighting techniques.

There are certain battles in life you will not win, be they physical confrontations or verbal attacks. This does not mean that you should abandon the path of the spiritual warrior.

There will be times when, due to your lack of physical preparedness or your standing in the hierarchy, you cannot emerge victorious. In such a situation, the spiritual warrior experiences the encounter and mentally notes what he can learn from it about the human body and human nature. Then, he continues to train himself both physically and mentally to achieve realization on the spiritual path as opposed to simply winning a battle. This does not mean that the person obsesses over the occurrence and continues to dwell on what took place. Instead, the conscious martial artist takes a certain period of time to reflect on the circumstances that led up to the occurrence, what took place, and how the confrontation ended in a less-than-favorable outcome. In this way, he delves into the nature of his own psyche and sees how he interacts with the world around him. Because the spiritual warrior does not live in a state of denial, he can make the situation a true learning experience.

Once the period of reflection has been accomplished, the spiritual warrior consciously lets go of the leftover negative emotions. In this way, he frees himself from fixation on the past and moves forward with new knowledge.

The average person will often find himself continually dwelling on the negative aspects of a losing experience. From this mind-set comes low self-esteem and a losing attitude. Just as all energy in the universe attracts like energy, a person who is lost in negative thoughts attracts negative experiences.

Victory

As is described in the theory of yin and yang, in all that is black there is a touch of white; this is also the case with defeat and victory. Defeat only happens when you do not learn and grow from the experience of losing. Thus, positive energy can come from negative. In victory, although it may feel better than defeat emotionally, there is still a negative aspect. Negative victory occurs when the victor relishes the winning experience and does not see it for what it is: simply the result of an occurrence. A negative victory is apparent when the loser is made to feel a long-standing sense of defeat. If this is the case, negative energy is formed and focused toward the victor.

If we study the lives of historical individuals who continually defeated or repressed others, we see that their lives usually ended in disaster or early death. This kind of misfortune is twofold. First, if a person lived in an environment in which she was surrounded by constant competition, he would have been challenged until he was finally defeated. Second, as he continually took pride in his victory over others, those he defeated held him in ill regard. As a result he was constantly bombarded by ill will; negative energy was continually focused in his direction. As those who take pride only in their victory never choose to consciously understand and master the energy of the universe, the negative energy builds up until they are eventu-

ally defeated by it; often it takes the form of sickness.

From egotistical victory is born conceit. From conceit is born carelessness. Carelessness gives rise to defeat.

"Live by the sword; die by the sword." There is no honor in defeating a person who does not wish to enter into battle with you. There is no glory in defeating an opponent who is not your equal in battle. For these reasons, the spiritual warrior never gloats in his victory. He understands that he simply took the appropriate actions at the appropriate time. He enters into the arena of competition only if his personal victory will benefit others.

Balance

Balance is a very profound element in the life of the spiritual warrior. Without a continued state of balance, enlightenment is not possible. When one leads a life out of balance with the ways of nature, one inadvertently attracts negative situations and encounters potentially harmful people.

Everyone can look at their own life and remember times when they may have felt lost, depressed, or self-destructive. During those times, we generally remember that we were either already surrounded by unhelpful people or we attracted people with similarly negative states of mind.

Because energy, both physical and emotional, is one of the most important elements in any martial artist's life, the spiritual warrior studies the way she interacts with the various forms of energy in the universe. This way she learns to recognize the arising of various factors that set her out of balance. The warrior's path is to develop the ability to consciously redirect negative energy before it damages her or someone else.

The first symptom of being out of balance with the ways of nature is emotional instability. This is often followed by physical illness. Throughout life, there are always emotional ups and downs. This is human nature. But becoming lost in emotional upheaval is what the spiritual warrior strives to avoid.

When one has fallen out of balance with nature, the first emotional experience is a sense of frustration. Frustration leads to a feeling of desperation. Desperation can lead to deep-rooted primitive emotions such as anxiety, fear, and anger. Anger has the potential of leading a person, especially a martial artist with advanced fighting ability, down a path that could end in causing physical and emotional damage to others. This path is never desirable. For this reason, the spiritual warrior must continually reflect upon her emotional state in order to recognize and cultivate a state of mind that is balanced and in harmony with the ways of nature.

The cause of a state of unbalance is the hardest thing for someone to see while they are going through it. Often, someone lost in this experience will be faced with a barrage of constantly shifting emotions. Engulfed in this emotional world, a person doesn't have much perspective.

Siddhartha Gautama, the Shakyamuni Buddha, profoundly stated, "The cause of suffering is desire." With this statement as a basis, we can immediately see that whatever unbalanced situation we may find ourselves in, it is based in desire.

Desire

Desire is at the base of all disharmony in this world.

Desire is, no doubt, one of the most subtle elements that drive us, for we humans intrinsically have desires. The question the spiritual warrior must continually ask himself is, "Why do I feel this specific desire and what will be the ramifications if I eventually get what I want?"

To the warrior, desire may be as simple as wanting to win a fighting match. You will often see boxers or kickboxers praying just before they enter their bout. Should God or the Universal Presence be involved in who wins a competitive fighting match? Most conscious martial artists would say no. Nonetheless, people believe that their desire to win is more worthy than their opponent's desire to win. Thus, they call on energy from external sources to help them to achieve their desire. This fixation on desire is what sets the individual out of balance.

The problem with living a life dominated by desire is that one desire gives birth to the next, and the next. Desires are limitless. The spiritual warrior maintains balance by keeping his desires in check and refraining from letting them control his life. Although all human beings experience desires, all are not controlled by them. Those who are not controlled by desire maintain balance in their lives and can thereby attain higher levels of understanding. Natural balance is never a product of fulfilled desires. It comes when we are at one with ourself, knowing what our body's and our life's true priorities are,

and then pursuing them mindfully.

The spiritual warrior who finds himself out of balance immediately refocuses on his physical training. This has been taught by martial artists for centuries, and now we know that aerobic activity releases positive hormones in the body and counteracts the effects of emotionally debilitating mental stress and depression. In addition, physical training clears the mind and the cognitive process benefits.

Along with physical training, the spiritual warrior performs a self-examination to determine which of his desires is causing his imbalance. When assessed, those desires are immediately left behind. If the thought of that desire arises again, it is consciously brought into clear focus in the mind and then released. By expelling the desire, he prevents it from penetrating his consciousness on a subliminal level and causing him additional loss of balance.

Finally, the spiritual warrior who finds himself out of balance with natural energy reemphasizes formal meditation techniques. He allows his mind to be calmed and moves his attention away from the distractions of the material world. In this way he realigns himself with the natural patterns of the universe. He maintains his balance when he aligns himself with his own natural patterns.

The Balance of the Warrior

Just because an accomplished martial artist has diplomas hanging on his wall and performs advanced fighting techniques, he does not necessarily embrace the refined spiritual understanding of the deeper realms of the martial arts. It is quite easy for a person to be drawn to the martial arts for the fighting and then never advance beyond that level of the art.

People are naturally drawn to the energy of either yin or yang. When you associate with one element too closely and you avoid the other, you lose your natural balance.

Many modern martial artists try to focus on only the yang energy aspect, the forceful, powerful, strong, masculine. As many martial arts styles emphasize excellence in physical fighting ability, the person who practices this style grows attached to the psychological gratification he gets from winning competitions and overpowering others. This person is concentrating too much on his yang energy. Although he may be adept at physical techniques, he should comtemplate his internal motivation.

A psychologically insecure person continually attempts to dominate others. The root of his problem may be in his childhood and upbringing. Unfortunately, an insecure person who finds his way into the martial arts can disguise his problem because his peers may respect his physical abilities. But the martial artist who trains in advanced physical skills without working on his inner development misses out on the spiritual development that is discovered with deeper study of the martial arts. These elements of the spiritual martial arts are open to everyone. People who are submerged in yang energy, however, are not the types who seek this understanding because its study shows that simply overpowering an opponent never reveals the answers to the larger questions of the universe. Simply because a martial artist has a high rank in his system and can perform fighting techniques competently, he does not necessarily deserve respect. Examine your teachers.

The balance of the energies of the universe is subtle. To become lost in one affects all areas of a person's life, from fighting to health and emotions. For this reason, the spiritual warrior is always aware of where he gets his emotional stimulation. If his happiness depends on defeating others, he knows he is not in accordance with the universal law of what is right.

The spiritual warrior objectively studies his internal motivations for all that he does; thus, he realizes his psychological shortcomings and areas of weakness. By recognizing his own shortcomings, he can work on improving the way he relates with his world.

Mental Imaging

Many modern teachers of metaphysics and martial arts instructors suggest that mental imaging, or visualization, is a good way to develop martial techniques. The ramifications of mental imagining must be clearly defined, however, if we are to use it to our advantage and to truly benefit the world.

Basically, mental imaging uses the same desirous energy as common desire. What is a mental image? The visualization of a situation or event occurring in a specific fashion, based on desire. For example, you may wish for a certain outcome in a competition. You may imagine yourself winning. Your visualizations are based in your mind, not in physical reality.

The problem with mental imaging is that the individual who does not achieve his visualized results comes to believe that he is visualizing incorrectly or without enough concentration. Thus, he either becomes disappointed with his own mental abilities or with the universal right because his desire was not met. This again raises the problem of desire. A desire, no matter how seemingly good, is still a desire.

The desire for anything in life to be more than it already is sets one on the path of karma (the law of cause and effect). On the path of karma there is always a winner and a loser. Where there are winners and losers, there is always competition. Competition always breeds disharmony. This is why spiritual masters teach that the universe is already perfect; all is as it should be. Nothing needs to be changed or improved.

This is where the large difference between the common martial artist and the spiritual warrior is obvious. The common martial artist dwells only in the world of the physical, where winning and losing are everything. The spiritual warrior, on the other hand, does not desire victory if victory offsets the natural balance of harmony in the world. The spiritual warrior must very consciously decide if he wishes to enter into the practice of mental imaging. If he does, he must do so very mindfully, taking extreme care that his mental imaging does not affect others negatively.

If these basic facts are understood, mental imaging can aid the martial artist when utilized consciously. To begin to understand this process, sit down and close your eyes. Relax for a moment or two and then begin to visualize yourself in your studio wearing your uniform. Watch yourself enter into a fighting stance. Now, as perfectly as is humanly possible, launch a front kick in your imagination. Feel every muscle in your body extend the kick to its perfection, as if you were actually performing it. Now, bring your leg back down to the floor, regaining your fighting position.

How did that experiment in mental imaging feel to you? Did you grow from it?

It is believed by some advanced martial arts instructors that by practicing techniques both physically and mentally on a daily basis, students can improve their style. To this end, they recommend that students take a few moments each day and mentally see themselves performing physical techniques.

If you desire to improve your physical skills, visualize yourself launching the perfect technique in various maneuvers. Remember that this training can only be used in close association with physical training or the muscles of the body will not develop the ability to perform what the mind commands.

Comparison

An element that must be considered when you use mental imaging is that of comparison. As a martial art practitioner you will continually see individuals who are stronger or more precise than you are. You may well wish to be as proficient in a specific technique as the person you witnessed, and through physical training you may well be able to achieve that level of competence. There will be certain moves, however, that you will never be able to master as well as someone else. This does not mean that they are a better martial artist than you are. It simply means that due to their body design they can perform a certain technique to a level of perfection that your body design does not allow.

Do not get lost in comparison. Develop your techniques to the most advanced level that you can. This is not to say do not strive to become a more proficient martial artist, but instead of comparing yourself with others, base your self-esteem on the skills you have and the good that you will accomplish.

Observation

The skill of observation is one of the primary tools the spiritual warrior embraces. Observation is not limited to perceiving what type of offensive techniques a sparring opponent or adversary is launching against you. Spiritual observation is much more refined than that. In your spiritual quest, you must be observant of all things around you. This is how you will understand how the warrior interacts with her environment and the universe around him and how he can use his surroundings to his own advantage in times of battle.

The first step in conscious observation is to come into intimate contact with the physical world around you. So many individuals pass through life never really taking notice of the world they are living in. This is in no small part due to the fact that many of us live in urban centers. We buy our food at supermarkets and have little need to interact with the external environment at all. This lifestyle breeds people who are deeply lost in their thoughts, about work, family, relationships, house payments—or the martial arts. The modern world keeps us removed from our environment, so the spiritual warrior must choose to interact with the world around him, even if it is an urban metropolis.

The Path to Reconnecting with the Environment

To begin your reintroduction to the world, step outside. What is the weather like: warm, cold? How does it make you feel? Is the sun out or is it cloudy? Study the sky. Are there any clouds? If so, what do they look like? Look at the color of the sky in relation to the color and shape of the clouds.

Allow yourself to see, feel, and experience the world as if you were doing it for the first time. Do not hold yourself to what you expect the temperature to feel like. Don't say to yourself, "I've seen a million clouds, I don't have time for this." Because life is lived in moments, you must take the time to experience each of them as fully as possible; life is short. Experience your world now, while you can.

The next step in your reintroduction to the world is to take a walk. With each step, how does the earth feel? Are you walking on cement? If, so, change your route and walk on the grass. How does it feel? How does the feeling you get from walking on grass compare to that of walking on cement? Do you get a different energy vibration?

As your walk continues, very

consciously open your eyes. What do you see? If you are walking in the woods, you see trees. Study them. What colors are the branches and the leaves? Perhaps you are walking along a seashore. Watch the waves come in and go out, observe their natural unending movement.

The countryside is not the only place where walks of consciousness can be taken. Living in an urban environment should not restrict you from walking. Moving through your neighborhood, what type of structures surround you? What are they constructed from, cement, steel, wood? Do these structures complement their surroundings? Do they interact with the natural environment, or do they detract from it? What conditions are these structures in? Do their owners take good care of them? What colors do you see?

Within all human creations there are a million levels of thought. Millions of years of human evolution went into the creation process of every man-made object you see. Any one of them can be studied and reflected on for a lifetime.

The spiritual warrior examines everything she feels, sees, and experiences. His own inner knowledge is deepened by her observations and his understanding of humankind's interaction with the universe is enhanced.

As your walk continues, study yourself. Are you comfortable or uncomfortable? In either case, what makes you feel this way? Is it conditions in your life, your interactions with other people, what you are anticipating will happen? All of these scenarios are not what is happening right now, as you walk. Allow any thought that comes to your mind, as you walk, to be a temporary wave that strikes the shore and then retreats back into the ocean. Let this walk, and what you experience on it, be all that occupies your mind.

Once you have let go of unnecessary thoughts, again study how your body feels in the process of walking. How does the temperature affect you? How does the movement of your walking make you feel? Take the time to determine for yourself why you feel comfort or discomfort in each particular condition.

The Personal Range of Comfort

We all have a limited range of temperatures at which we feel most comfortable. This is not only determined by where you grew up and by where you live now, but also from what you have come to like and dislike.

What you will experience on this and other conscious walks is that there is a specific type of weather temperature you feel best in. This is natural. What the spiritual warrior strives to do is expand her range of comfort. He learns how to be comfortable in a widening range of climates and temperatures. In this way, the spiritual warrior learns to drop the limited perspective of good and bad, comfortable or uncomfortable, that the average person experiences every day.

The way the temperature comfort range is expanded is to first take very careful notice of the external temperature. Then, study your body reaction to it. In your mind, you have control of your bodily sensations, so simply allow yourself to not be bothered by the heat or the cold. If it is very hot, visualize all of the heat leaving you while telling your body that you feel cool. If it is very cold, let your inner warmth emanate and feel your body temperature rise. Of course, in extreme conditions of cold other methods of warming the body must be used. But through this practice you will discover that so many of our perceptions are in the realm of personal taste and desire, instead of direct experience.

Human Interaction

Finally, on your walk, begin to notice the people around you. What are they wearing? How do they walk? Do their faces have looks of peace or anxiety? Notice how their bodies move. Is there a correlation between the way a person is dressed and the expression on his face? Does the clothing he wears affect how he interacts with others and how others interact with him?

As each culture and subculture within a society has a specific way of dressing in accordance with how people see themselves and how they present themselves to others, there is no way to tell what kind of person someone is by looking at the way he is dressed. Nonetheless, when you observe a person dressed in a fashion that seems to feel appropriate for him, you notice confidence in his step. This may be the case with the soldier and the police officer in uniform because they take pride in their life's role. This confidence may also be seen in a monk wearing his robes, or a martial artist wearing his black belt, or an adolescent wearing the fashion of the day. This is your environment, this is your world, this is your lifetime; don't let it pass without coming to know it intimately.

Many budding spiritual warriors find it difficult to sit down and consciously turn off their thoughts and enter into a meditative state of mind. The conscious walking exercise is a good introduction for the individual who has not previously studied mind-refining exercises or meditation techniques.

By first allowing your mind to focus on what your body is experiencing and then coming to an understanding of the various physical feelings and emotions you are having, you can move into a naturally meditative mind frame. Once you begin formal consciousness training, your mind will naturally connect with your body and the expansive world of energy around you.

Focusing

Focusing is one of the most important elements of training for the spiritual warrior. At the most fundamental level of martial training, the student is taught to make random strikes at punching and kicking bags or hand-held striking gloves to refine his physical focusing techniques. These targets are generally large, as the novice student has not yet developed striking precision. With time, the student becomes more proficient and a smaller striking target is used as the student learns to hit more precisely.

Focus training also includes performing a set pattern of movements involving punches, kicks, and blocks. These patterns are commonly referred to by the Japanese word *kata*. These basic focusing drills are designed for the novice and the highly trained martial artist alike to refine their combative techniques and continue to develop body and mind alignment. There is, however, a much deeper level to focus training than is presented on the surface.

To the spiritual warrior, focusing takes on a much deeper meaning when the application of these drills is taken to the realm of meditation. Just as the Zen Buddhist nun who walks one step and then kneels down and bows—only to stand up and take one more step before her next bow—is using movement as a means of meditation, so is the martial artist who sees the techniques as a means for insight into his own movement, but also as a means for merging his energy with the moving energy of the universe.

Movement as a meditation technique allows the spiritual warrior to refine his offensive and defensive tactics, and it allows him to observe how the various martial arts techniques impact other objects. Striking a hanging bag, compared to hitting a fixed target like a *makiwara*, creates a very different reaction—for the martial artist and the object itself. Additionally, making contact with a moving focus glove is a very different feeling than kicking into the air.

Each martial art technique has a specific reaction in relation to what type of target it impacts. Not only do objects react to strike force in calculable ways, the human body reacts in certain ways to the various objects—animate or inanimate—it makes contact with. Therefore, the first level of meditative focus is on impact reaction. Once this is understood, he no longer needs to calculate what type of offensive or defensive technique is appropriate in a given circumstance. Instead, he will know what to do without thinking. Combat will no longer be a thinking process; in essence, it will become a meditation.

At the beginning levels of this movement meditation, the spiritual warrior practices a very basic technique, such as a straight punch or a front kick. He will first locate an imaginary target in the air near his body. He then launches the move very slowly, noting each muscle movement.

As the fist or foot moves toward its strike point, he studies how it feels as her body extends to make imaginary contact.

This style of movement meditation should be practiced for at least ten repetitions at the outset of each training session, with basic techniques such as the straight punch, the front kick, the side kick, and the roundhouse kick. These moves form the basis for the more advanced martial arts techniques, and if they are practiced properly, the more advanced techniques will be mastered correctly.

The next level of meditative focus training is to locate a physical object to strike—this may be a hanging bag, makiwara, or the like. It is best at the initial stages of training to perform your striking technique to a free standing object, because a training partner can inadvertently distract your focus.

Again, begin with a basic technique and strike outward at the object very slowly, noting each of your muscles' movements as your body progresses toward its target. Do not hit the target with force, instead just allow your body to touch it.

How does the impact point of your body feel when it makes contact with the target? Reflect on this as you leave your strike point in place for a time.

Once you get the basics of this focusing meditation, you can move on to faster movements against different targets—independently standing or held by an opponent. Additionally, if the situation presents itself, you may also spar with a training partner to come to understand how your body reacts to targeting a human. Generally, this style of training is less meditative because a human training opponent might be distracting. However, by experiencing how each movement feels, you will grow in your understanding of the spiritual martial arts.

3
THE MEDITATION
OF THE
SPIRITUAL WARRIOR

The practice of meditation has been handed down for centuries as a means of mental and spiritual development. Throughout history, meditation has been practiced and refined by monks of various spiritual orders to gain a glimpse of the eternal. Over time, the meditation techniques once known only to holy men have become available to everyone. The practices once available only to those who lived in spiritual reclusion are now procurable by all who seek them.

Meditation is a sacred process. It is the method used by the spiritual war-rior to calm the mind and to connect the body and mind with the infinite. For these reasons, meditation is never taken lightly; it is entered into with a clear understanding that it is a means through which to communicate with the cosmic realms of this universe.

The spiritual warrior's initial intro-duction to meditation often begins when he first embarks on the practice of martial arts. At the beginning of his martial arts training, the individual becomes so engulfed in the learning of each new technique that his mind does not have time to concentrate on anything else. This focused concentration is the first level of meditation, for the mind is locked onto a singular object, a specific physical movement.

With time, however, the martial arts novice becomes more proficient in the techniques and the movements that comprise his system of self-defense. With elementary proficiency generally comes a state of broader awareness; the practitioner no longer needs to focus as acutely on his techniques. The physical techniques have become repetitive and can be performed naturally.

This unconscious shift from mindful concentration to relaxed, natural action is what sets the spiritual warrior apart from the average martial artist. The spiritual warrior never executes a movement or physical technique mindlessly and just because he believes he knows how to do it. The spiritual warrior understands that each time any physical movement is performed, it is never like the time before. You may have taken millions of steps in your life and most of them may have been exactly the same as the last, but there is that one occasion when, for no apparent reason, you take a step and you slip and fall. The reason this occurred is a lack of awareness.

Meditation is not an activity one generally simply begins. It is for this reason that prescribed meditation techniques have been outlined for the average person to develop the ability to focus his mind precisely on and to raise his mind to a level of communication with the infinite.

Beginning to Meditate

Meditation leads to stillness of the mind. Many people do not understand the concept of stillness of mind. They falsely believe that the still mind of meditation is similar to that of sleep. Meditation is not sleep. Meditation is the conscious focusing of the mind on a singular object to bring about a state of refined consciousness. From this refined consciousness, the mind no longer travels in a million directions, the way it habitually does, bounding from one thought to the next. Instead, the mind becomes still and cosmic understanding is born.

The Four Stages of Meditation

There are four stages of meditation in Mahayana Buddhism:

1. The focusing of the mind

2. The purification of the mind
3. Calming the mind
4. Enlightenment

The first stage, focusing the mind, involves focusing, or concentration. This is achieved by developing the ability to stop random thoughts, fueled by emotions, from dominating the thought process. This first stage of meditation is achieved by concentrating the mind on a singular object.

The second stage of meditation involves the purification of the mind. Purification of the mind is achieved by the spiritual warrior who follows the Eightfold Path of Buddhism and is not lured into unnecessary emotional and physical entanglements.

This second stage of meditation, purifying the mind, is the first step to selflessness. Selflessness removes the constrains of emotion and ego from the decision-making process, allowing one to move through life with purpose.

The third stage of meditation invokes mental calming. Calming the mind brings the experience of stillness. Stillness is the experience of no-thought. No-thought allows the spiritual warrior to replenish his body and mind with universal peace.

This third stage is achieved when it is no longer necessary to focus on a meditative object with the thinking mind. This occurs when the mind experiences *muga*. Muga is the state in which the mind becomes unified with the cosmic whole and cannot be disturbed.

The fourth stage of meditation is linking with Buddha-mind, satori.

Preparing to Meditate

The spiritual warrior experiences the various stages of meditation seated in zazen and also while performing martial art techniques. Seated meditation is easier than meditation associated with movement because the body is still, therefore there are fewer distractions. For this reason, a firm foundation in zazen must be established before the spiritual warrior can effectively assimilate martial art movements into his meditative understanding.

The Process of Mental Refinement

Meditation requires instruction and training. Since the time of our birth most of us have embraced the mind-set of the fast-paced modern world, and our minds jump from one momentary thought or emotion onto the next. We never really notice this until we attempt to meditate and calm our thoughts, then we immediately realize that at the outset it is almost impossible to not have a thought jump into our minds. This is not bad, it is simply the way most of us have learned to encounter life—via the thinking mind. Meditation techniques have been designed to slowly guide the thinking mind away from the need for a new thought every few seconds and toward the stillness of Buddha-mind. To this end, the science of breath control is utilized as the first step in learning how to slow and ultimately control the thinking mind.

Breath Control

Ancient breath control techniques are known in Japanese by the term *kokyuho*, or more commonly by the Sanskrit word, *pranayama*. *Prana* is translated as "the breath that gives life," for without breath life would not exist. *Yama* is "control of." Thus, pranayama is the control of the life-giving breath.

All advanced martial artists understand that breath is used in all martial art techniques. Using conscious breathing, one is able to maintain control over one's energy level while in com-

bat. Just as a weightlifter exhales as he lifts a heavy weight, the martial artist exhales as a powerful offensive or defensive technique is unleashed. The reason for this is that if force is powerfully released from the body while the intake of breath is in motion, that breath becomes locked in the body and causes strain to the entire metabolic system. Therefore, the breath is exhaled with each release of energy.

The martial artist who is trained in ki knowledge also understands that ki is closely related to the breath. It enters the body with the intake of breath and exits the body with the out breath. Therefore, conscious breath control is fundamental to the development of the spiritual warrior.

The Three Objectives of Breath Control

Breath control serves three purposes in meditation. First, it consciously focuses the mind of the practitioner on the single most important life-giving function—breathing. Second, pranayama cleanses the body by oxygenating the blood while eliminating waste products brought in to the body by breathing unclean air. Finally, through highly refined practices, pranayama links the spiritual warrior to the source of unlimited energy, ki. Therefore, the practice of breath control is fundamental to the advancement of the martial artist.

Breathing Meditation

The first level of learning how to meditate involves breath control. Meditative breath control brings the mind into a state of calm. With the mindful inhaling and exhaling of breath, the spiritual warrior raises breathing from a necessary life function to a technique that links the thinking mind to Buddha-mind.

Preparing for Meditative Breath Control

All forms of meditation are entered into ceremoniously. This is the case whether it is formal zazen or preparatory introductions to meditation such as breath control.

The first step the meditative practitioner must take to begin zazen is to be seated in the appropriate posture. Whereas, the yogi uses the cross-legged, lotus position—*kekka fuza* in Japanese or *padma asana* in Sanskrit—to perform his meditation practices, the martial artist uses *seiza*, a kneeling posture (figure 1).

The reason the kneeling posture is

Figure 1

preferred by martial artists is that it doesn't lock the body into a sitting position. The martial artist must be able to standup instantly in case of danger. The kneeling posture allows her to do this. Additionally, the kneeling posture places the body in the shape of a pyramid. With the spine erect, this causes the naturally flowing ki to localize in the skull, thus aiding the practitioner in deepened meditation and enhanced energy retention.

The kneeling posture is achieved by first allowing your left knee to slowly drop to the ground, as your right knee bends to accommodate this movement. You then direct your left foot to extend outward, behind you, bracing the top of this foot against the floor. Your right knee then slowly lowers to the ground and your right foot follows the same pattern of extending backward. Your knees should have approximately one foot of space between them. You place the big toe of your right foot on top of the big toe of your left foot and straighten your spine.

Not everyone can comfortably remain seated in the kneeling posture for an extended period of time. As meditation should never be a painful process, if it's too uncomfortable, simply sit in a chair with your spine erect to perform any of the exercises described in this book.

Hokkai In

In the various forms of seated meditation you will form your hands into a *mudra*. A mudra is a formal gesture made with the hands in order to keep the ki energy from escaping from your body.

The mudra commonly used with zazen is known as *hokkai in*. This mudra is made by laying your left hand in your lap, palm up. Your right hand then lies on top of your left fingers. You then lightly hold your left thumb, forming a loose fist with your right hand.

Breathing Observation Exercise

Assume the kneeling posture. Form your hands into the hokkai in. Partially close your eyes, keeping a soft focus on the floor approximately two feet in front of your knees. Breathe naturally for a few moments as your mind calms down. Now, as you are breathing life-giving air in through your nose, begin to witness the air entering your body. Begin to take a very conscious notice of how the process of breathing this life-giving force into your body makes you feel. Each person has her own experience of this feeling.

Once you have completed your first natural in breath, consciously exhale all of the air in your lungs slowly through your nose. Feel this life-giving force leave your body. Once all of the air is out of your lungs, contract a bit harder on the muscles of your upper abdomen and you will feel that there is a slight amount of air left, which then leaves your body. Once you have expelled all of the air in your body, do not immediately breath in new air. Experience this lack of air.

Once you feel it is time for you to breathe again, consciously bring in air through your nose. Do not stop this incoming breath until your lungs are full of air. In fact, once they feel full, breath in just a bit more air and feel how they still slightly expand.

If you are breathing correctly, your stomach cavity will expand as this in breath is drawn. Some people have developed the wrong method of breathing, generally in their childhood, and their stomach cavity actually contracts as they breath in. If you find this happening to you, now is the time to stop that incorrect practice altogether because by breathing in this way you unconsciously restrict your lungs and do not allow your body to take in all the necessary oxygen to nourish your body. If you discover this is the case, and you find yourself breathing incorrectly, this breathing exercise will help you to teach yourself the correct breathing practice. If you find that you are breathing normally, and your stomach does expand as breath comes in, continue to breathe in this natural fashion.

Once your lungs have filled with air, feel their fullness, consciously under-

stand that this air is what gives you energy and life. Without it, you would first become weak and then would die.

People who breathe shallowly have limited energy. Those who breathe fully possess an abundance of energy. This can easily be seen in people who regularly partake of aerobic exercise, be it running, bicycling, swimming, dancing, or martial arts. In all of these cases, these people possess an abundance of energy. Why? Because they regularly allow their body to breathe deeply and fully. Those who do not exercise allow their breath to become more and more shallow with each passing year, so their energy is depleted as they get older.

With this understanding in mind, again exhale completely through your nose. Once your lungs feel empty, again embrace the emptiness for a moment. Then, as you breathe in, observe where your in breath naturally expands in your body. Is it deep into your abdomen or is it only as far as your chest? If the latter is the case, you are not taking full advantage of all the natural energy that is available to you.

If you watch the breathing of a newborn baby, you can see it go deeply into the abdomen. In a person who is near death only the chest expands. From this point on, consciously expand your abdomen when you breathe.

As you continue to practice this breath observation exercise, inhale each breath slowly and naturally and, allow it to fill your lungs. Then hold the breath deeply for a moment. As each breath is exhaled, allow all of the air to leave your body.

Normally, you breathe and never think about it. As you practice this breathing exercise, allow yourself the time to appreciate the divine perfection of the breathing process.

Focusing on inhaling and exhaling is one of the most basic meditation techniques. Although basic, it is a very precise way for you to link your body and mind with the universal suchness of your inner being.

Figure 2a

Nerve-Calming Breathing Exercise

The nerve-calming breathing exercise, known as *nada suddhi* in Sanskrit, is the breath-control technique you can use before your sitting meditation when you will not be using your breath as your primary meditative focus or when you find your mind is agitated. This breath-control technique is mentally calming and prepares the mind to enter into meditation more readily.

In kneeling posture, bring your right hand up to your nose and close off your right nostril with your thumb (figure 2a). Breathe in slowly, yet deeply, through the left side of your nose. Observe your breath enter and slowly flow to your abdomen. Once the breath has been fully taken in, allow it to remain for at least five seconds. Now, open your right nostril by removing your thumb, and then close your left nostril (figure 2a). Allow the breath to flow from your abdomen out

Figure 2b

Figure 2c

through your right nostril, naturally. Once your breath has completely exited, feel the serene emptiness. When it is again time to breathe in, take the breath in through your right nostril. Hold it in your abdomen. When the time to release comes, close off your right nostril with your thumb, opening your left nostril (figure 2c), allowing the breath to exit via your left nostril. Repeat this process approximately twenty times.

Energy Channels

There are subtle channels of energy running through the body and affecting the human nervous system; they are known as *nadis*. Like the meridians, if the nadis become blocked, illness occurs. Pranayama cleanses these energy channels, keeping them free from blockage. Of the nadis, the *sushumma* is most important. This current runs along the spine and maintains the body's overall ability to process, utilize, and disperse ki. On each side of the sushumma are individual nadis. The *Pingla* current runs along the left side of the spine and is accessed via the breath through the right nostril. The *Ida* current runs along the right side of the spine and is accessed via the breath through the left nostril.

The Pingla current is warming and the Ida current is cooling. When you practice nada suddhi, you stimulate each current in turn, warming and then cooling the body. This stimulation balances the two currents, linking the energy of yin and yang in your body. When this practice is performed, the body is brought to a state of harmony and the mind is relaxed.

To demonstrate for yourself the warming and cooling energies of these two currents, you can try a simple experiment. When you find yourself cold at night, sleep on your left side. This will cause your body to naturally breathe through the right nostril. Thus, the Pingla current is activated and the body is warmed. The opposite is true if you find yourself warm at night. Sleep on your right side and you will activate the cooling Ida current.

Through the practice of nada suddhi, you prepare your mind for formal meditation.

Meditation

Meditation should never be a complicated process. The essence of meditation is simplicity. In zazen, emptiness is embraced. To this end, we use only a few necessary ancient preparatory techniques.

Meditation is not a timed technique. Many beginning practitioners believe that if a thought comes to their mind, or they are not able to hold their focus for more than a few moments, they are somehow unworthy and incapable of achieving a deeply refined level of meditation. This is not the case.

For the spiritual warrior, conscious movement in connection with universal energy is the goal of meditation. The spiritual warrior is not seeking meditation to become a drug, he uses it to link his body and mind with universal spiritual understanding. As is understood in Zen, enlightenment is instantaneous. The individual mind can be prevented from this immediate realization only by the belief that one is not already enlightened. Therefore, the time one spends meditating does not determine his level of spiritual achievement.

Satori comes to the spiritual warrior from his conscious integration of body, mind, and spirit. Satori is never perceived as a method of escape. As the Japanese proverb goes, "Prior to enlightenment chop wood, carry water. After enlightenment chop wood, carry water."

This being understood, the thinking mind can, nonetheless, be calmed through the continued practice of meditation techniques. Therefore, it is to the advantage of the martial artist to take the time to calm the mind in order to glimpse the stillness of makoto.

The Basis for Meditation

At the base of formal meditation is the practice of precisely focusing your attention. This quality of meditation is known as *dyrana* (concentration) in Sanskrit. This level of concentration is often first experienced by the novice martial artist as he becomes deeply involved in his physical techniques. Once the basic physical techniques have been absorbed, however, they no longer provide the advancing martial artist with the necessary level of challenge. Thus, a state of concentration must be consciously invoked.

Precisely focused attention is a rarity in this world. We all are bombarded by a million images and trained to think innumerable thoughts at one time. The practice of precise concentration teaches the spiritual warrior to develop acutely focused attention and to place his mind in a certain mental location in order to consciously remove herself from such things as physical pain or emotional obsession.

For the spiritual warrior to develop the ability to lock his mind onto a single object, he must practice for a period of time. Concentration exercises are the first step in the process of refining the mental focus of the warrior.

The first step in developing the ability to focus precisely is to be able to turn off external stimulaion from your mind. This is a practiced ability and is not accomplished overnight.

One, Two Breathing

In zazen, the practitioner begins to develop his meditative techniques by taking the breath observation exercise one step farther. Kneel in seiza, hands in hokkai in, and close your eyes. Begin to focus your attention on your breath. Breathe naturally, allowing your breath to enter and exit your body without any thought of controlling it. Once you have reached a relative state of calm, with each in breath, mentally count "one." As your breath naturally exits your body, count "two." Each in breath, one. Out breath, two.

If you find your concentration being pulled away to a thought, do not become angry with yourself—thinking is a natural process. Instead, refocus your attention on your breath, counting "one, two."

Mentally counting, in association with breathing, helps you to maintain your concentration on something other than the random thoughts of your mind. This technique, although it seems elementary, focuses your mind and links your body to its life force, air. For this reason, various schools of Buddhism use this breath-counting meditation method as their main practice of zazen.

The Gazing Exercise

The gazing exercise, *thratakam*, teaches you to open your eyes and focus on a single object. The ideal object of focus differs among spiritual traditions. Hindus will often gaze at a statue of the deity. Tibetan Buddhists use a *thangka* (a painting of divine images), or mandala. For a martial artist, a more appropriate object of concentration might be a lighted candle, an object that has its own source of energy. As described in the *Nei Ching*, fire is one of the primary elements of life. Additionally, fire is a force unto itself. Fire is never stagnant; it is in constant movement, therefore fire is a source of power.

In the case of a lighted candle, the motion of the fire is confined to the flame burning atop the wick. The very slight movement of the flame will help your mind to remain still at the initial stages of the gazing exercise.

Concentrate on the movement of the flame. Embrace its power. From this concentration exercise, your ability to remain focused on whatever task is at hand will be enhanced.

The purpose of the gazing exercise is to set an amount of time for yourself to practice focusing your attention. In the early stages, you may only wish to perform this exercise for five minutes, so you don't wear yourself out. During this five minutes, however, you should try to control your thoughts and not allow them to wander. If a thought about anything comes to your mind, simply let it pass away. Don't force it; just allow it to flow outward, like a wave that has struck the shore and is now returning to the ocean.

As you practice this concentration technique you may want to gradually extend the period of time you focus on the candle. At first, thoughts will come to your mind. With practice, the random thoughts will stay away for longer periods of time. Ideally, you will extend this exercise from five minutes to fifteen minutes. Once you have reached the fifteen-minute point with few or no thoughts, you will find that you are developing the self-discipline to focus your attention on any of life's activities, even those you don't enjoy.

Formal Meditation

The practice of meditation, *dyana* in Sanskrit, is the next step of spiritual development after concentration. Concentration allows you to focus your mind. In meditation you first focus your mind, then relax into communion with the absolute.

To begin the formal meditation practice, first assume the seiza kneeling posture. Next, focus on the life-giving breath. This is ideally accomplished by first consciously taking a few deep breaths and then performing nada suddhi, the nerve-calming breathing exercise. Once your mind has been initially calmed, form the hokkai in mudra with your hands and begin to witness the floating random thoughts in your mind. Watch them fly away like white doves flying into a pale blue sky.

Next focus on a specific meditative image. As a technique of meditative focusing, the ancient Hindus and Buddhists practiced focusing on a single sound. This sound is called a mantra. A mantra is a single word or phrase that possesses divine essence. The syllable *om* is a universal mantra.

Om is the sound representing the never-ending universal vibration. In Japanese this is known as *parasbda*, primal sound. By invoking *om* in your mind, you can connect into the divine vibration of the universe. This is an ideal mantra to use while practicing your meditation.

What you actually choose to use as a focus for your meditation is entirely up to you. Whatever point of focus you choose, however, must remain constant throughout your meditation. What you will come to experience through the continued practice of meditation is that whatever image you use will come to emanate from your being. As you think, so shall you be.

Now that you have prepared yourself, begin to focus on this chosen sound or image. Allow your mind to embrace it fully. If you are using a mantra, with each in breath repeat it silently in your mind, then with each out breath think it again. Continue this process with each breath throughout your session. Do not allow thoughts about jobs, relationships, or the winning of martial arts tournaments to engage your mind.

Do not attempt to force yourself to sit in meditation for long periods of time at first. Give yourself five minutes or so. As you progress with this practice, you will naturally begin to meditate for longer periods of time.

The formal practice of zazen should be done twice a day, in the morning and at night before sleep, for a comfortable amount of time. In addition, zazen should be practiced just before martial arts training and just after.

As your mind becomes more centered, you will be able to enter formal meditation at will. Moreover, meditation will become an integral part of your being; all of your actions will become more and more the practice of meditation. No longer will you simply take out the trash to take out the trash; you will begin to see each action as an action that helps you to recognize the divine perfection of this universe. Through mediation you will come to be an interactive part of the universe, instead of simply being a sole entity, unaware of the all-pervasive oneness.

Often a martial artist believes that she does not need to meditate, that her physical training is all that is required. Without mental discipline complete mastery of the body and mind is impossible.

The Physical Benefits of Meditation

The benefits of concentration and meditation can be applied to everyday circumstances, once the basic techniques are mastered. By being able to focus on a mental image, you will find that you are not easily caught up in negative life experiences that may occur. This type of inner concentration will help you to keep your mind clear and focused when you are experiencing physical pain, for example, or perhaps when you are distracted by feeling too cold or too hot. These are just a few very basic examples, but this method of advanced concentration is applicable to all types of circumstances.

It is very important to remember that when practicing this type of mental concentration, the spiritual warrior never chooses to remove himself from life events. Life is life, and that is that. Experiencing life is what your physical being is all about. If negative experiences continue to follow you, this is a good indicator that you should refocus and redefine your life instead of running away from it. Nonetheless, at times we all encounter situations of physical discomfort. The ability to control your mental state can help you in these times.

To achieve this level of concentration, the first step, as with all mental refinement practices, is to focus on your breath. Witness your breath and control it. Do not allow it to become too shallow or rapid, as often happens in times of physical trauma.

Once you have stabilized your breath, immediately assess your situation—which you would probably prefer to ignore. You may be too cold, too hot, just cut by a knife, have just broken a bone, or perhaps you are having a dentist drill on your teeth. Quickly detail every element of what is taking place and how your body is reacting to it. Once you have noted the physical reactions to the external stimuli, go to that level of concentration that you have experienced in your meditation practice. Place an appropriate image in your mind. If you are cold, you may wish to see yourself on a warm beach. Let the cold leave your body as the warmth of your mind embraces you. If you are too hot, let the heat flow out of your body as you see yourself swimming in cool water. If you have been injured, take your thoughts away from the injury, go to a place in your mind where you allow yourself to forget the current pain as you remember an experience of peace, happiness, and joy.

It is important to remember to never allow yourself to become too lost in mental imaging. Use it as a tool. Control it, as opposed to being controlled by it. Do not allow it to remove you from reality, like a drug. This is your life; live it, experience it, do not hide from it for long periods of time, as this never leads to enlightenment.

Movement Meditation

Mitama shizume means to "polish the soul through activity." The spiritual warrior uses the physical techniques of his system of martial arts to take himself deeper into the realms of meditation, forming a conscious link to the divine through the movements of his body.

Walking Meditation
Walking meditation, known in Japanese as *kinhin*, is the first level of movement meditation upon which the spiritual warrior focuses. As this is the introductory level of meditation used in association with physical movement,

Figure 3

force muscle tension into your hand when forming the fist because that causes undo concentration to be placed on a singular part of your body. With your next in breath raise this fist to the level of your solar plexus. Exhale naturally, then, as you take in your next breath, take your right hand and wrap it over your left fist (figure 3).

Allow your hands to remain naturally in this position for a few natural breath cycles. When your mind is centered again, open your eyes and cast your gaze approximately six feet in front of you. Breathe in this sight. See everything as if it were the first time. Breathe naturally for a few cycles. With your next in breath, take a half-step with your left foot. Mentally observe the experience of movement: your foot lifts up from the ground and then touches down again. Feel the miracle of this action. With your next in breath, move your right foot a half-step forward. Experience the meditative perfection of this movement.

Kinhin is very methodical. It trains the meditative mind to move in association with the body. With each in breath, move forward, with each out breath rest. As you move forward, if you encounter a wall or an obstacle, turn to your right and continue your

it is performed very slowly. The mind is allowed to remain in a meditative state and not become unduly distracted by the body's movement.

To perform kinhin, stand naturally with your spine erect. Close your eyes and begin to observe yourself naturally breathing for a few moments. When your mind has become centered, slowly form your left hand into a loose fist. This should take the same amount of time as one natural in breath. Do not movement. This movement is always clockwise, symbolizing the constant movement of the universe.

Kinhin should be performed for approximately fifteen minutes when you first begin this practice. It can be performed indoors or outdoors in any location you find peaceful.

Kinhin should not be undertaken with another person. Everyone has a different height and body construction and a different concept of movement, and the way in which someone else moves may affect the naturalness of your meditative movement.

Kinhin will teach you that meditation can be practiced while moving. This is the first step in training your body and mind in the methods of moving meditation.

Iaido

Iaido (*iai* means "to draw" and *do* means "way"), is the meditative art of drawing and sheathing the sword. When Zen Buddhism was practiced by samurai, the meditative understandings of Zen also crossed over into the art of warfare. As the sword was one of the primary weapons used, it became a central focus of advanced physical meditation.

The predecessor to Iaido was *Iai jutsu,* which was created by Hojo Haya-shizaki Jinnosuke Shinenobu in 1560. This art of meditative sword fighting was developed to kill the opponent swiftly and precisely. The art was refined in the eighteenth century by Eishin, when samurai warfare was on the decline. The meditative art then took on the form in which it is practiced today: drawing the sword, striking an imaginary target, and then returning the sword to its sheath.

There are twenty movements of precisely removing the sword from its sheath and fifty slicing techniques in Iaido. The ability to remove the sword and cut with perfection, to the exact specification of these techniques, is the meditation for the practitioner of Iaido.

The exactness associated with Iaido teaches the modern spiritual warrior that mastery of a technique is not something that can be achieved in days, weeks, or even months. Mastery takes a lifetime. For this reason, the spiritual warrior never claims mastery of a technique, instead she releases herself from the bounds of ego and continues to refine and redevelop her understanding.

Kyudo

Kyudo (the way of the bow) is another highly refined meditation associated with the martial arts. The bow and arrow were some of the earliest weapons. Kyudo, in its original application known as *Kyu jutsu* (technique of archery), was considered the most important of the eighteen methods of warfare detailed in the sixteenth century text, *Kakuto-bugei*. *Kakuto-begei* outlined the Japanese techniques of warfare and was required study for all bushi.

Over time, Kyudo transcended into the realms of a meditative science. Proficiency in shooting an arrow into a target was no longer enough for a person to be considered a master of the bow. Simply shooting an arrow skillfully is known as *noshahichu*. Shooting an arrow with right-mind, however, is known as *seishichu*.

The practitioner of Kyudo progresses over three levels of mastery until the way of the bow leads one to satori. The difference between these three levels is known as *tekichu*. Tekichu defines how the archer is able to hit her target, either through physical or spiritual mastery.

The first level is *toteki*. At this level the archer can hit the target with her arrow. Although she may be physically proficient, she possesses no divine inspiration in her movements and is unaware of the meditative nature of archery.

The second level is *kanteki*. The archer, through repeated practice, breath control, and mental mastery, can pierce the target with her arrow, as opposed to simply hitting it.

The third level of Kyudo is called *zaiteki*. At zaiteki the archer becomes one with the target. No longer is the target an object. Instead, it is another manifestation of the self. At this level, the arrow does not travel to the target but instead exists in the target.

Ku

Physical meditation leads one to the state of mind known as *ku*, emptiness. Ku occurs when one has perfected the technique of his weapon or his martial movement and from this meditative perfection he is raised to the level of the cosmic experience of emptiness.

Ku exists when no thought of action is taken. The action occurs in its own perfection, yet the mind does not have to define what physical movement must be made to achieve the action, nor what will occur when the action is taking place or has been completed.

Ku is not a state of the thinking mind. Ku is a product of the meditative mind that has been linked, through physical action, to the cosmic suchness of the universe.

Ku is not accomplished by the martial artist who is able to perform a technique sufficiently to do it without thinking about it. This is achieved by repetition, not meditation. The reasonably accomplished martial artist can perform various techniques competently with little or no thought. Yet, the same martial artist will be mentally distracted by the first interesting image that presents itself to him.

Ku is achieved by the spiritual warrior who, through precise meditative practices, comes to embrace the essence of his martial art movements and can then unleash that essence as a process of cosmic perfection. In this state no thought of the individual self is present. The mind of the spiritual warrior is in cosmic communion so that he is not distracted by external stimuli or unbalanced by the ultimate outcome of his actions. In fact, he holds no desire whatsoever for any specific outcome. Thus, his action is made at the heart of meditation.

Ku cannot be desired and then achieved. It cannot be practiced for. Ku is a manifestation of satori; it happens and then it is.

Meditation and the Modern Martial Arts

The modern martial artist can make any technique in her system of self-defense an experience in meditation. It is the mental preparation that goes into the process of performing the technique that makes it meditative. The spiritual warrior can gain tremendous insight into the movements of his body and his mind by precisely concentrating on physical techniques. The next step, once the mind of the spiritual warrior has been suitably processed with zazen, is to link the physical mind with the divine mind through martial arts techniques.

For the process of movement to become meditative, the spiritual warrior must exist in *ima* (the now). He does not wish to change the past because she understands the concept of divine perfection. The future has not yet happened, so he does not ponder possible outcomes. Each movement he makes is with complete awareness, not allowing his mind to wander to random thoughts. Thus, every movement becomes a meditation.

The process by which you can transform your martial arts practice session into movement meditation is a fourfold path. First, choose a basic technique:

this can be a straight punch, a low front kick, or any technique that is not excessively elaborate. Once you have chosen the technique, master its basic application. If you do not possess physical mastery over the technique, you cannot expect meditative mind to occur, as you will be distracted by the physical performance of the technique. Once you achieve basic physical competency, you can move on to the second level of movement meditation, namely, focusing your mind with pranayama and zazen. Once your mind is in the appropriate state, move on to the third level by beginning to slowly perform your chosen technique. As you do so, observe how your body feels with each movement the technique requires. How do your muscles feel? What is the experience of your arm or your leg extending? And so on. Once you have defined the physical aspects of your techniques, change the focus of your mind and move to the fourth and final level of movement meditation: as you perform your chosen technique, witness it as a movement in accordance with the overall perfection of the universe.

In movement meditation your thinking mind enters the meditative mind. It uses your movements as a vehicle. Only you can meditate, no one can give you the meditative mind-set.

4
KI: INTERNAL AND EXTERNAL POWER

The understanding of ki was first documented in China over two thousand years ago. This knowledge moved to Korea, Japan, and then the rest of the world. Ki is the unceasing energy that fuels our universe. The person who has an understanding of how ki can be harnessed has the ability to utilize this ever-present energy in times of mental or physical need.

The undisciplined use of ki can be illustrated by stories like that of an average person remarkably lifting a fallen refrigerator off a loved one. This average individual is able to somehow harness superhuman power and save the other's life. Through the practice of ki development exercises, the martial artist can learn how to harness this energy—which is in abundant supply throughout the universe—and channel it.

The development and understanding of ki is not only a way to tap into superior physical power, but it is a method for focusing mental strength as well. By focusing ki, an individual can possess a much clearer perception of the world around him, and he can pinpoint his mental energies to achieve whatever mental task is at hand.

Ki is not only available to reclusive holy men who live in mountain caves.

Ki is available to anyone who consciously focuses his body and mind and comes into harmony with universal energy. Ki is not a mystical power that enables the practitioner to perform superhuman feats of destruction upon another human being, although many Asian films and charlatans have depicted this to be the case. Knowledge of ki does, however, substantially aid an individual in his or her self-defense abilities.

The reason ki is helpful to one's self-defense is twofold. First, the ki practitioner understands how ki energy flows endlessly throughout the universe and how it enters the willing, unhindered body in unlimited supply. From this, the martial artist becomes a conscious participant of this strength and energy. Second, the advanced martial artist understands how ki moves along the meridian pathways of the human body. From this knowledge, the ki practitioner possesses the ability to strike an attacking opponent at vital pressure points, *kyusho* in Japanese, or *kup sul* in Korean, disrupting the flow of ki in the opponent's body. This style of self-defense leads the spiritual warrior to a heightened ability to overcome even the strongest adversary.

The use of ki energy is generally only practiced at the advanced level of martial arts. This is because the body and its functions must first be well understood and then the mind of the practitioner must be focused before true ki science can be mastered.

PHYSICAL STRENGTH VERSUS KI

Physical strength and muscle development are body enhancements that are easily achieved with exercises and weightlifting. This type of strength development is, however, quickly lost when the exercises are discontinued. Muscle development is, therefore, a temporary form of strength.

The person who develops internal strength through the use of ki, on the other hand, never loses his understanding of how to effectively access ki. So this form of internal strength and energy is always available to him.

Exaggerated muscle development is believed by some to be a way to become more physically attractive. This type of superficial attitude can be attributed to low self-esteem. The majority of those people who choose to attack other people for money and physical gratification have been proven to suffer from this same sense of low self-esteem. Those individuals who prey on other people are often the same ones who seek to overdevelop their bodies instead of their minds.

To enter into blow-by-blow combat with one of these individuals, on a physical level, is not to your advantage. By doing so, you lower yourself to the level of animal. This is why the spiritual warrior uses his understanding of ki when he needs to defend himself.

THE FOUNDATIONS OF KI SCIENCE

Ki, or internal energy, was first written about in the Chinese text, *Huang Ti Nei Ching* Su *Wen* (The Yellow Emperor's Classic of Internal Medicine.) This text is commonly referred to as the *Nei Ching*.

In the *Nei Ching*, ki is described as the universal energy that nourishes and sustains all life. It flows through the universe and through each individual. An abundant, unrestricted flow of ki in the body keeps one healthy, whereas a diminished or impeded flow of ki can lead to illness.

UNDERSTANDING KI IN THE HUMAN BODY

Ki flows through the human body along invisible circulation channels known as meridians. There are a total of twelve primary, or constant, meridians. These twelve meridians are referred to as "constant" because ki energy circulates through them in a continual path. Ten of these meridians are defined by, and govern, specific organs of the human body: the gall bladder meridian, the liver meridian, the lungs meridian, the large intestine meridian, the stomach meridian, the spleen/pancreas meridian, the heart meridian, the small intestine meridian, the bladder meridian, and the kidney meridian. The other two constant meridians, the heart constrictor meridian and the triple warmer meridian, are related to the control of bodily functions. The heart constrictor meridian governs the continual flow of blood throughout the body, and the triple warmer meridian controls the energy of respiration.

Each of the constant meridians has branches on both the right side and the left side of the body. Ki flow along the meridians is therefore directed exactly to the specific regions or organs of the body the meridian affects. Furthermore, if a person experiences a blockage of ki flow along any of the constant meridians, precise stimulation can be applied to reinstate proper ki circulation.

There are two other meridians that also aid in the control and circulation of ki through the body. They are the conceptual meridian and the governing vessel meridian. As they do not have direct relationships to specific organs and are not integral elements of the body's primary ki circulatory system, they are referred to as secondary meridians. These secondary meridians influence specific ki channels and bodily activities.

Ki flows in a constant and unchanging direction, either ascending or descending. Each of the meridians is dominated by either yin or yang and one of the five elements: fire, earth, metal, water, and wood.

PRESSURE POINTS

Kyusho, pressure points, are precise access sites along a meridian. Kyusho, when properly stimulated with acupuncture needles or accupressure, enhances the flow of ki along a specified meridian. Thus, applying pressure to kyusho aids the body in recovering from ki blockage or ki deficiency.

Likewise, if kyusho are hit with a precise offensive strike, called *atemi,* they can also hamper the flow of ki in an individual. And with this understanding of pressure points, the martial artist can begin to utilize ki in the realm of self-defense.

THE BASIS OF KI SELF-DEFENSE

For the spiritual warrior to effectively utilize ki at will, she must possess astute mental focus, developed through zazen, and understanding of how ki works within the human body. The spiritual warrior is in command of the three elements that control ki in the human body: spirit, essence, and breath.

To utilize ki in self-defense, one must have an abundance of ki. The martial artist who is known to be strong in ki is referred to as *tsuyoki.* One who is weak in ki is known as *yowaki.*

Ki Gong (ki skill) is the first step in attaining the ability to consciously focus ki for external use. Ki Gong is initially accomplished through concentration on the center point. The center point is generally referred to, in the martial arts world, by the Japanese term *hara.*

The Center Point

The hara or *tanden* (burning place of energy) is the center of balance in the human body. It is additionally the location where ki energy gathers.

The hara is located approximately four inches below the navel and extends two inches in each direction from this central point. This location is the source point of all usable ki in the

Figure 4a

Figure 4b

human form and is therefore a very special part of the body.

The martial arts practitioner who wants to use ki energy efficiently must first find her hara. This can be done by performing the center point defining exercise and the opening and closing exercise.

Center Point Defining Exercise

Stand with your legs approximately shoulder-width apart. Bend your knees slightly. Your feet should be pointing forward. Bend your elbows slightly. Extend your fingers so that your hands are natural and at your sides. Allow your fingers to be semi-relaxed and naturally separated. Bring your hands in front of your center point. Form an inverted triangle with approximately one inch of space between your thumbs and forefingers (figure 4a).

Once you have achieved this stance, close your eyes and breathe slowly and deeply. Allow your breath to go deep into your abdomen. Once you

Figure 4c

Figure 4d

achieve a relative state of calm, after approximately ten natural breaths, begin to visualize the location of your center point.

Now, pivot your wrists, until your open palms face upward. Bring your fingers together and point them toward each other (figure 4b). Breathe deeply in through your nose and visualize your breath entering your body in a golden flow through your nose and finding its way to your center point. As you perform this exercise, bring your hands

slowly up your body to chest level (figure 4c).

Once you have taken in a full breath, hold it in naturally for a moment. Embrace its golden essence and power as it gathers in your center point. Now, release it and pivot your palms to a downward position (figure 4d). Allow the golden breath to leave your body naturally. See it flow from your center point and exit through your nose. Observe this as your hands move down to their original position

Figure 4e

Figure 5a

(figure 4e).

Using this exercise, the exact location of your center point will become clear and you will develop the ability to easily direct ki throughout your body. You should perform this center point breathing technique at least ten times, any time you need to refocus your body, mind, or ki energy.

The Opening and Closing Exercise

The cosmic mudra of opening and closing not only focuses the mind on the location of the hara but is a movement meditation that synchronizes the movements of the body with the breath, thus forming a conscious link to the meditative mind.

To perform this exercise, stand with your legs about shoulder-width apart. Bend your knees slightly. Your feet should be pointing forward. Bend your elbows slightly, allowing your arms to fall naturally at your sides. Extend your fingers. Do not tighten the muscles of your hand, but allow your fingers to be

Figure 5b

Figure 5c

semi-relaxed and naturally separated.

Close your eyes and begin to observe your breath as it enters your body naturally. Observe the in-flow and the flowing out of your breath for a few moments. When you feel comfortable in your standing position and your mind is calm, begin to visualize ki entering your body through your breath in a golden flow. Watch it entering through your nose and moving to your hara. With each in breath, see the golden flow of ki enter your body, filling

your hara with ki energy. With each out breath witness the exhaled ki flood your surroundings with golden ki energy.

Now, bring your hands up into prayer position in front of your face (figure 5a). Observe three complete breath cycles of golden ki energy entering your body. As you exhale your third breath, bring your hands above your head, allowing your thumbs and your first fingers to touch; your other fingers are extended naturally (figure 5b). With your next in breath, mentally say

Figure 5d

Figure 5e

the mantra, *om* as you make a broad circle with your arms extended, moving down in front of your hara (figures 5c and 5d). With the out breath move your hands above your head again. With each new in breath, repeat *om*, as your hands move down to your hara (figure 5e). With each out breath move your hands above your head again.

This exercise should be performed approximately ten times a day as a way to define your hara and to link your body and mind with cosmic infinite energy. Once your hara is clearly located, this exercise can be performed as a movement meditation to consciously link your body and mind with the universal ki force entering your body and gathering in your hara.

The Four-Phase Ki Breath Exercise

Once your hara is clearly defined, you can take ki breath control practice to the next level to consciously link the intake of ki to your breath. Begin by being seated in seiza, kneeling posture. Focus your mind by watching your natural breathing pattern for a few moments.

You will now begin the technique known as the four-phase breath control exercise. The four-phase breath control exercise is accomplished by first inhaling deeply in a continuous flow through your nose. Allow the intake of breath to be silent. Never force the intake of breath; this causes only resistance from the body. As in the previous *aum no kokyu* exercise, visualize ki entering your body in the form of golden light with each in breath. Allow the breath to fill your lungs. Witness the ki reaching to your hara and illuminating this region.

Once your intake of air is naturally complete, allow this ki breath to remain in your body. Do not exhale it immediately. Instead, witness the ki, in the form of golden light, emanating from your hara and engulfing your being.

When you feel it is time to exhale, do not allow the ki breath to leave your body in a broken flow. This disrupts the natural pattern of ki. Let your breath exit in a natural continuous flow.

As your breath leaves your body, visualize any impurities in your body leaving you with the exhalation. All

that remains is pure golden ki light.

Once you have completely exhaled, do not attempt to immediately refill your lungs. This may take a bit of practice, for many people panic from the initial feeling of needing to breathe. Instead of immediately breathing, feel how light your body has become with the absence of air. Observe the emptiness and the purity it possesses. When it becomes necessary to breathe, do so. Allow the consciousness of ki to again enter your body.

The four-phase breath exercise can be used, as described, to enhance ki visualization and circulation in your body. When you first begin to use this ki breath control method, allow each phase to last approximately five seconds, or whatever amount of time feels natural to your body. At the outset, do not attempt to hold any phase longer than you feel comfortable with, as this can cause you to disrupt the natural flow of ki in and out of your body (and may even cause you to pass out). As you continue with your further development of ki energy, however, you will find, due to the increased amount of ki energy circulating throughout your body, that the time period of each phase of this breath control will naturally increase until each phase may last as long as one minute.

Ki-oriented *kokyuho* (breath techniques), such as the previously described aum no kokyu and the four-phase breath exercise, train the subconscious levels of your mind that ki enters your body through breath. Thus, through breathing in this manner, access to ki is unlimited. From this understanding, the martial artist brings his body and mind to a new level of cohesive interrelationship with universal ki energy.

The Center Point and Ki Self-Defense

Once you locate your hara, all ki-orientated strikes and self-defense applications are accomplished by initially focusing on this center point. The Japanese syllables *ki ai*, or Korean *ki hap*, means the meeting together of energy. These words are what martial artists yell with the unleashing of energy. The yell is an expression of the practitioner pulling ki up from the hara and then releasing it with the execution of a technique.

Figure 6a

Figure 6b

EXTENDING YOUR KI IN SELF-DEFENSE

The first level of ki self-defense to be mastered is how to effectively extend your ki. By extending your ki in a directed fashion, you can add enormous power to any self-defense technique you employ.

Ki Breath Movement Exercise

Assume a natural standing position and breathe naturally for a few moments, meditatively observing your breath. Then, perform the four-phase breath control exercise for a repetition of five four-phase breaths.

With your in breath, pivot your palms upward at your waist level (figure 6a). As your breath comes in, visualize ki entering your body and traveling to your hara. As your ki breath comes in, bring your palms upward until they are at your head level (figure 6b).

With the completion of your in breath, hold them in position for five seconds. Visualize ki emanating from

Figure 6c

Figure 6d

your hara and traveling up your body, through your arms to your hands. Then, as you exhale, pivot your body so you are facing the opposite direction from which you began (figure 6c), invert your palms so they are facing downward (figure 6d), and slowly lower them to the ground in time with your breath (figure 6e). As you do so, visualize the golden ki energy emanating from your palms.

When you are ready to take your next in breath, repeat these five steps (figures 6f–6i), again pivoting around to return to your original position, shown in figure 6a.

This Ki breath control exercise can be perfomed for a maximum of seven repetitions a day to train your body to feel how ki can enter and exit your being with the naturalness of slow meditative movements.

Figure 6e

Figure 6f

Figure 6g

Figure 6h

Figure 6i

Figure 7a

Figure 7b

Boulder Push Exercise

Begin in a standing position, with your hands loosely at your sides. Focus your attention and begin to breath very consciously, watching your breath move from your nose into your center point in a golden flow. Once you feel calm and have a good sense of your hara, move your hands into ready position—in fists in front of your hara (figure 7a). Then take a fresh breath through your nose and move your left leg forward, as if you were about to take a step. Remember to hold your attention on your breath entering your nose in a golden flow, and then moving to your hara. This breath enters as you take your step. As you step, bend both of your elbows slightly and turn your wrists until your open palms are facing upward, at approximately your waist level.

Once your intake of breath is complete, hold the golden breath locked in your hara. Feel the ki energy radiate as you bring your upward-facing palms up

Figure 7c

Figure 7d

the side of your body to your chest level (figure 7b). Once at chest level, turn your open palms outward and face front (figure 7c).

As you exhale, tighten all of the muscles of your shoulders, back, arms, and hands. Powerfully push forward with your open palms, visualizing the golden ki energy exiting your palms and pushing up against a large boulder in front of you (figure 7d). Witness your ki energy entering and moving the boulder with the power of your push. As you extend your arms, keep your left

arm slightly out in front of your right arm while pushing forward.

Once your breath is completely exhaled, observe the emptiness for a moment, as your arms remain extended. Feel the ki radiating from them.

When it's time to take a new breath, breathe in a golden ki breath and slowly return to your original standing position with your hands loosely at your sides. When the breath is complete, feel how full of ki your arms and hands have become. Allow the breath to exit naturally, feeling the ki remaining.

When it's time to take your next breath, step forward with your right leg this time, and perform the same exercise on your right side.

The boulder push exercise is ideal for gathering ki into your arms, shoulders, and hands when you are anticipating the need to perform strenuous movements. This exercise stimulates the meridians of these limbs providing additional ki power to them.

As you practice these two extension exercises, witness how first the upper part of your arm, then your lower arm, and finally your hand and fingers begin to feel more and more strength with each out breath that travels from your hara out to your fingers. Experience the strength your hand feels as ki energy radiates from your fingers.

Once you begin to feel the power and energy that you have directed to your hands with these two ki extension exercises, you can begin to focus and then extend this same ki energy from any part of your body. Simply focus your mind, concentrate on your hara, and breathe your ki energy into any location in your body.

The Straight Punch

As all martial artists understand, it may be necessary at times to strike out aggressively at an attacking opponent. If you allow the wild emotion of the moment and the force of adrenalin to guide your defense, you cannot consciously take control of the altercation. For this reason, the spiritual warrior learns to consciously extend ki while striking out in times of battle.

The first form of a forward offensive strike, which most novice martial artists are taught, is how to deliver the straight punch. The straight punch is a refined punching technique, because it follows a very linear path to its target. It is a very rapid striking technique, and successfully blocking this style of punch is complicated.

The basic straight punch is launched from the front stance. A front stance is accomplished by extending your right leg forward a couple of feet in front of your left leg. Your forward knee is bent and your rear leg remains straight. Your front foot faces straight ahead and your back foot should be at a forty-five-degree angle. Once you have achieved this position, find a natural balance with approximately 70 percent of your weight on your front leg and 30 percent on your back leg.

Once in the front stance, form your hands into fists. Reach your left hand slightly out in front of your body with your fist parallel to the ground. Place your right hand at waist level with your fist facing upward.

Figure 8

parallel to the ground (figure 8).

It is important not to practice the ki-oriented straight punch rapidly, as if you were in an actual confrontation. In fact, it is better to perform it slowly in the beginning, as this gives you the ability to consciously observe the entire movement of your punch: how it is extended, how your muscles react, and how you can best stay balanced while performing it. This way, you will become much more consciously aware of how your body feels as the straight punching motion is taking place.

To take the straight punch to the level of a ki technique, it must be performed in conscious association with your breath. Therefore, settle into the front stance and take a few deep breaths, watching the golden ki breath enter your nose and proceed to your hara. Once you are focused, begin the punching technique. As you do so, exhale the golden ki energy that you have stored in your hara and visualize this ki energy extending from your hara, up through your body, and along your arm. As your punch reaches its climax, see the golden ki energy forcefully extending from your fist into an imaginary target in front of you.

This type of ki extension practice is not limited to the straight punch. According to your own martial arts

To begin the straight punch, slowly extend your right fist forward, directly in front of you. As its name implies, the straight punch travels straight ahead to its target, which, in this case, is at solar plexus height, and in the middle of your chest.

As you are performing this forward punch, bring your left hand back to hip level. As your fists move, they pivot at the wrists, so your retreating fist turns back to an inverted position as your punching fist finishes its movement abilities, you can associate it with any punching, kicking, or grappling technique you like. The ultimate goal of this type of ki extension training is to allow you to become very aware of the way that ki can emanate from any part of your body. In a case of self-defense, you can focus and utilize your ki, consciously directing it to an exact location on your opponent's body.

Striking to Intercept Ki

There are many locations on the human body that offer direct access to ki meridian path (see page 93). These kyusho can be hit to interrupt the flow of ki in an attacking opponent. By striking precisely to a kyusho, you can effectively stop the ki flow along a specific meridian. When the flow of ki is stopped in a specific meridian, your opponent's offensive abilities will be hindered.

Striking to a pressure point does not necessarily immediately knock a person out or cause a body part to become numb, as is taught by some martial arts charlatans. What this type of self-defense does achieve, however, is the interruption of the overall ki force in an attacker. This type of self-defense is analagous to a body part falling asleep when blood circulation is blocked.

When applying forced pressure to a specific pressure point, your goal is not to magically render your opponent lifeless. What you are planning to achieve is both short-term and long-term interruption of your attacker's ki energy.

In the advanced martial arts, a focused pressure-point strike is initially accomplished by focusing your energy in your hara, then, as your strike travels toward its pressure-point target, you expel your focused ki, with a ki ai shout, and strike your opponent at one of these precise locations. His ki will be interrupted, and you can continue on with additional self-defense as necessary.

Pressure Point Strike Locations

The pressure points that are ideally accessed by a single strike are the top of the skull, the central forehead, behind the ear, the back of the jaw bone, the central chest, the ribs, and the top of the hand.

1. **Top of the skull** This is a pressure point of the gall bladder, liver, bladder, and governing vessel meridians. Striking it disorients the opponent by interrupting ki circulation to the brain.

2. **Central forehead** This is a pressure

point for the gall bladder, bladder, triple warmer, and governing vessel meridians. By striking it, you will severely disorient your opponent. The disorientation will last for several minutes, in which time you can leave the scene of the attack or continue with additional self-defense as necessary.

3. **Behind the Ear** If you feel with your finger behind the back of your ear you will notice a slight protrusion of bone. This is a pressure point for the gall bladder and triple warmer meridians. This pressure point additionally affects the functioning of the inner ear. As the inner ear directly affects balance, striking this location will cause your opponent to lose his balance and become disoriented.

4. **Jaw Bone** The pressure point for the jaw bone is located at the point where the jaw arches, exactly where the jaw bone curves and extends out toward the chin. This pressure point also affects the functioning of the inner ear, thus the balance of the opponent. It is also a pressure point for the stomach, the small intestine, and the triple warmer meridians. Striking it disorients your adversary and affects his balance.

5. **Central, upper chest** This pressure point is located on the sternum (the long flat chest bone that joins the ribs). Its exact location is approximately one inch above the solar plexus. It is a pressure point of the kidney and conceptual meridians. Due to its close proximity to the heart and the lungs, striking it sets the opponent's breathing off balance. He will breathe sporadically for approximately two minutes, or longer, depending on the power of the strike.

6. **Ribs** With your finger tips follow your ribs from the center of your body to your side, applying slight pressure. You will immediately feel a pressure point when you come to the under side of a rib. This is the pressure point you desire to locate when in combat. This is the point for the gall bladder, liver, stomach, and the spleen meridians. All of these meridians, in one form or another, affect the flow of blood throughout the human body. By striking to this location, the blood flow of the individual is substantially interrupted.

7. **Top of the hand** Located at the exact center of the top of the hand,

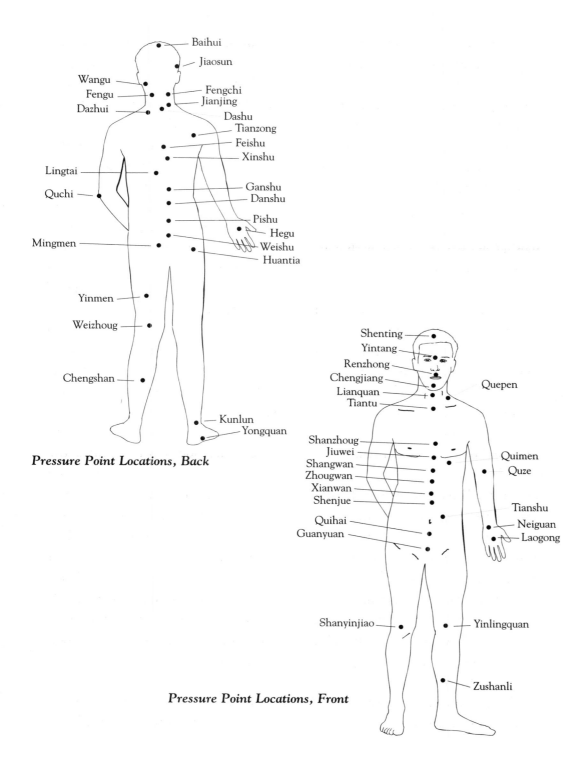

Baihui
Jiaosun
Wangu
Fengu
Dazhui
Fengchi
Jianjing
Dashu
Tianzong
Feishu
Xinshu
Lingtai
Quchi
Ganshu
Danshu
Pishu
Hegu
Mingmen
Weishu
Huantia
Yinmen
Weizhoug
Chengshan
Kunlun
Yongquan

Pressure Point Locations, Back

Shenting
Yintang
Renzhong
Chengjiang
Lianquan
Tiantu
Quepen
Shanzhoug
Jiuwei
Shangwan
Zhougwan
Xianwan
Shenjue
Quimen
Quze
Quihai
Guanyuan
Tianshu
Neiguan
Laogong
Shanyinjiao
Yinlingquan
Zushanli

Pressure Point Locations, Front

in between the bones leading to the middle and third fingers, this point is for the triple warmer meridian. By striking him there, you make your adversary's hand go numb.

It is important to keep in mind when you strike to these pressure points you are not attempting to simply win the battle in a one-strike victory, as a force-oriented martial artist may hope to do by striking the knee joint or the temples of an opponent. To strike any of these precise locations disrupts the ki flow of the attacker and inflicts momentary pain.

When the spiritual warrior uses ki interruption techniques for self-defense, he does not have time to locate a specific pressure point the way an accupressurist would when applying healing touch therapy. Similarly, he does not generally have the time to hold a pressure point for more than a few seconds. It is for this reason that a martial artist must not only possess an exact understanding of meridian pressure points to make ki self-defense effective, he also must be able to strike or apply debilitating pressure rapidly and precisely.

As the spiritual warrior never enters into battle with thoughts of annihilating the opponent, these strikes serve as a warning to the adversary of what is to come if he continues his attack. If the attack does continue, by striking these preliminary strike points you have disrupted the opponent's ki flow so that overtaking him should be easier.

NONFORCEFUL KI INTERRUPTION

The ki of an attacker is not only interrupted by forceful striking techniques. In fact, the more advanced martial artist will not focus his defense on offensive techniques at all. Instead, he will choose to interrupt the ki of his opponent by far less obvious methods. In many cases, he may apply direct pressure to one or more of his opponent's pressure points with a holding or a grabbing technique.

An easily accessible point is on the inside of the elbow. To locate this pressure point, reach across your body with your thumb and apply pressure to the inside of your elbow. After a moment or two you will begin to feel a strange sensation in your lower arm. What you have done is inhibited the flow of ki along the lung, heart, and heart constrictor meridians. Your arm will begin to feel numb. Over a longer period of applied pressure your breathing will be inhibited.

This point is an ideal place to locate on an attacker who has grabbed hold of you. Of course, this type of self-defense is not as instant and dynamic as a powerful striking technique (which can also be unleashed to this location in the form of a knuckle strike). But as each self-defense situation is defined by its own limitations, simply applying focused dynamic ki pressure to this pressure point may be the exact type of defense that is called for.

Another self-defense pressure point is located at the central point of the neck. With your middle finger, follow the clavicle or collar bone down the front of your neck until you reach its central point. There you will feel a skeletal V formation. At the central region of your neck, apply pressure downward, as if you were pushing inside, behind this bone. (Note: this pressure point is located on both sides of the forward neck). Hold pressure there for a few moments and your breath will begin to be interrupted. Held over longer periods of time, the pressure will severely disrupt breathing.

The third of these locations is the jaw bone pressure point, located where the jaw bone curves. This pressure point is very close to the one discussed in the previous section. With your fingers follow your jaw bone down from your ear to the point where it arches out toward your chin. Now, apply pressure and push in behind the bone. You will immediately feel the pressure point. This pressure point is ideal when you want to quietly, yet forcefully, shove an attacker away. This pressure point affects the inner ear, so long-term pressure to it will cause an attacker to lose his balance.

It is important to remember that ki does not have a physical manifestation like the growth of a muscle when it's flexed during weightlifting. Ki is a mental science. Just as positive thoughts have been proven to have a beneficial affect on all aspects of physical and mental well-being, ki energy derives its strength from this same source—the positive mental energy of your mind.

Sound waves cannot be seen, yet they are experienced. Allow the ki to flow outward from your fingers as a sound speaker sends out music into the environment. Mentally observe the ki energy flowing from your fingers as it dissolves into the atmosphere around you.

5

REFINING THE PHYSICAL DISCIPLINES

From the study of the meditative arts in association with physical movement, the spiritual warrior comes to understand how the body moves most efficiently within itself, in accordance with others, and in association with nature and the universe. Although no spiritual warrior ever wants to enter a fight, at the root of martial arts is the ability to successfully defend oneself if the necessity arises.

CIRCULAR MOTION

The Earth is essentially round. It constantly rotates in a circular pattern on its axis. All of the other planets in our solar system are also round. They each rotate on their own individual axes and constantly move around the Sun. This pattern of repeated, completed circles is what the spiritual warrior looks to as a means for developing individual martial perfection.

From a geometrical perspective, the circle is constant. There is no beginning or end to it. The spiritual warrior who meditates on this concludes that the circle is whole, nonending, complete within itself and in a constant state of motion. The spiritual warrior understands that to remain in harmony with this universe, all movement should be circular.

Applied to Self-Defense

The spiritual warrior knows that the best way to defeat any aggressive opponent is not to meet force with force but, instead, to deflect and redirect the offensive energy of the opponent with the most appropriate, least aggressive method possible. The spiritual warrior uses circular motion to intercept an opponent's linear attack. In addition, he uses linear offensive striking techniques to penetrate an opponent's circular defense. In either case, the understanding of circular ideology is paramount to the spiritual warrior's self-defense strategy.

The spiritual warrior envisions himself being surrounded by three concentric circles. These circles are set at three-foot intervals and define his range of defense. By initially defining where you are in relation to your opponent, you will stipulate what type of defensive or offensive action needs to be taken.

At the center of any circle is its axis, *jiku*. For this reason, the axis theory must be understood before the student can move to the more advanced level of conscious self-defense, which utilizes the three concentric circles theory.

The Axis Principle

The pivotal point of any circle is its axis. The axis is a circle's central point of rotation, therefore it is its source of movement and balance. Each person has an internal axis. You can imagine the internal axis as an imaginary line starting just above your head, running through your body, and exiting between your legs. This imaginary axis line is your body's standing center of rotation. It is instrumental for balance and all forms of self-defense.

The internal axis principle is not like an imaginary back brace that keeps your body unnaturally erect. Instead, it serves to remind you of the necessary alignment you need to maintain while practicing the circle theory of defense. If you do not feel 100 percent fluid and in balance, your internal axis is out of alignment.

The internal axis principle allows the advanced martial artist to remain in a natural stance during combat, as opposed to the formal stances such as the front stance, the horse stance, or the back stance, commonly associated with traditional martial arts. The reason the spiritual warrior chooses to avoid the traditional stances is that they are too rigid and hinder him from achieving a continuum of fluid motion.

The internal axis is fundamental to advanced defensive applications. When you're defending yourself against an aggressive opponent, you strive to throw him off the balance point of his axis. If you do, he easily comes under your control, and you can effortlessly bring him to the ground.

When you begin training with the axis theory, you should always practice with mindfulness of your internal axis. As you progress, you should extend this axis consciousness to all of your physical movements. From both of these practices you will gain a deepened understanding of how your body moves. As your axis understanding becomes an integral part of your movement consciousness, you will no longer need to think about it. Instead, it will be an innate part of all of your actions, and all your self-defense techniques will be launched from a position of perfect balance.

Pivoting on the Axis

From a standing position, allow your forward lead foot to anchor your placement on the ground. With this foot as your stationary guide, you can rotate your body in any direction you desire. Try this by allowing your body to pivot lightly on the ball of this foot, while your rear leg glides in a circular rotation around your current position.

Your lower arms should be extended outward, away from the front of your body. Your elbows remain bent and are lifted approximately six inches away from your torso. Your fingers should be outstretched, and your hands loose. While performing this pivoting exercise keep your body and mind in a relaxed, yet aware state. By remaining in this relaxed state while performing the exercise, you do not waste unnecessary energy.

When you pivot in this fashion, you allow your body to prepare to launch backward or forward if an opponent were to attack you. By allowing your arms to remain in a natural state, you will be able to effortlessly launch them into appropriate defensive maneuvers if the need arises.

Pivoting on Your Axis with an Opponent

The second phase of this exercise is to perform it in the same way with an opponent encircling you. The opponent should be instructed to launch safe attacks at you from various positions in your ongoing turn. He should not tell you what type of attack he is launching, as that type of traditional martial arts training allows you to be mentally prepared with the most appropriate defense. A street confrontation is never like that. You must learn how to defend against random attacks if you hope to be a competent warrior.

From this exercise, you will gain an understanding of opponent awareness and how to successfully deal with the various attacks an adversary may launch at you in a street encounter. From performing this exercise with an opponent, you will learn how to react instantly to the oncoming advances of an attacker. Instant reaction is a must for a martial artist to be an effective street combatant.

Through practice with the two pivoting-on-the-axis exercises, you will begin to notice that you are no longer aware of only what is directly in front of your eyes. Instead, you begin to become increasingly aware of objects that appear in your peripheral vision. Your ability to notice and judge the intentions of oncoming opponents will be greatly increased.

The Primary Circle

The spiritual warrior visualizes three concentric circles around his body when evaluating appropriate self-defense action. The first circle you need to become aware of is the primary circle. This circle extends approximately three feet, or the length of your extended arms, around your body.

The primary circle is the most important circle to define in self-defense because it is your safety zone. If an opponent penetrates your primary circle, this is the time you must take appropriate self-defense measures. If an adversary does not move in that close, you are not in immediate danger so no physical confrontation is necessary.

Defining your primary circle does not mean that you remain stagnant and don't move from within a certain area. What it does mean is that you have an effective space around your body that defines what type of defensive actions will be necessary for you to take. The primary circle moves as your body moves.

The primary circle defines a necessary defensive range, in addition to delineating where you can launch effective offensive techniques. If you attempt to stretch your basic techniques and move outside of this approximate three-foot range, you will overextend your body, exposing vital areas, and leave yourself in a prime position to be counterattacked by an accomplished opponent.

If you find it necessary to move beyond the primary circle to unleash an offensive technique, you should do so by relocating your entire body and closing the distance between your opponent and yourself, instead of attempting to elongate your basic punching or kicking technique, haphazardly endeavoring to reach him.

The Secondary Circle

The secondary circle is the area that is between three and six feet around your body. At this distance, you cannot easily reach your opponent with basic techniques. Therefore, if combat is eminent, you must move toward him.

How you arrive at the secondary circle is paramount, for if you simply charge in at a competent opponent he will use your aggressive force to his own advantage and disable you. To keep this from happening, you must be able to travel to an opponent as fluidly as possible.

The Linear Forward Motion Drill
Stand in a very loose fighting stance, your fists at chest level. Very consciously, move rapidly forward toward an imaginary target approximately four feet away

The best way to travel this distance is to push out from your back leg. Bend your back knee very slightly and then propel yourself forward as your front leg rises slightly and moves along the ground. You do not want this knee-bending motion to become obvious, because the trained opponent will see it and react accordingly. Therefore, practice so that your propulsion is very subtle.

As you arrive at your new defensive spot, do so with your hands still in fight-ready positioning at your chest. This will allow you to be ready to successfully defend against any type of attack your opponent launches.

By moving forward in this fashion, you keep your body weight predominantly on your back leg—approximately 75 percent. The weight on your lead-in leg is about 25 percent. The reason for this is twofold. As the lead-in leg is closest to your opponent, by keeping your weight off it, you avoid being taken by surprise by a successful sweep kick or lower-leg roundhouse kick. If your opponent does attempt a kick to your lead-in leg, you simply allow his force to drive through it. Although your leg may be hit, you won't lose your balance because you don't resist his kick. You can simply realign your balance and stance. Your opponent, on the other hand, will have delivered a forceful, noneffective offensive technique, leaving himself open to an effective counterstrike.

The second reason to leave most of your body weight off your lead-in leg is that by doing so you can quickly launch it into a powerful kicking technique after you close the distance. By keeping your weight on your rear leg, your lead-in leg is free to maintain body balance.

The Tertiary Circle

The tertiary circle is from six to nine feet away (figure 9a). Traveling this distance to engage your opponent should never be necessary unless he has a weapon—like a gun—which you cannot run from. Never move directly toward an opponent at this distance unless it is absolutely necessary for your survival.

To move in from this distance successfully, you must move very rapidly, yet maintain your bodily integrity in doing so. Your opponent will obviously be aware of any oncoming movement you make at this distance. Therefore, the ideal way to travel this

Figure 9a

Figure 9b

Figure 9c

distance is in an offensive posture.

Offensive techniques like the stepping side kick or the jumping side kick are highly effective at this range (figures 9b and 9c).

The opposite from moving toward your opponent is when she advances at you through the secondary and tertiary circles. In this case you have the advantage because she is moving in toward you. As she covers the distance, you have the chance to get ready.

Figure 10a

Figure 10b

SPHERICAL MOVEMENT

Spherical movement means that in defensive and offensive applications, the practitioner realigns his placement from his opponent's direction of convergence instead of meeting it head on.

Have your opponent straight punch toward your face (figure 10a). At the instant his motion begins, slide around, inside his punch (figure 10b). What you notice is that you do not get hit.

Try the same exercise with the added element of counterattack. Again, your

Figure 10c

Figure 10d

opponent straight punches at you; you move around inside his attack (figure 10c). You will witness that, being inside of his attack, his head and body are open for a counterstrike, which you can accomplish with a straight punch of your own (figure 10d).

Some systems of self-defense teach you to retreat backward from the oncoming straight punch. This method however, is only advisable under certain circumstances. The problem with this style of retreat-oriented defense is that by stepping straight back you may well avoid an offensive attack but to counterattack you will have to move back in, on the same line your opponent is advancing forward on. This allows him to prepare for a second attack. For this reason the spiritual warrior is taught that it is more efficient to encircle your opponent, avoiding his attacks, than to make linear retreats and advances.

You can expand on this exercise by fluidly moving from one side to the other of your opponent's attacking techniques, be they punches or kicks. When you try this you will see that by moving in a crescent shape in front of your opponent, away from his attacks, you will avoid being hit. You will also come to understand how best to avoid each type of attack.

The Circle and the Gate

In any confrontational situation, the martial practitioner visualizes a primary circle around his body. Your opponent has this primary circle surrounding his body as well, whether he chooses to visualize it or not. If you and your opponent recklessly go hand-to-hand, you stand the chance of becoming needlessly injured. To keep this from occurring, the spiritual warrior takes into consideration the various elements in play such as his opponent's ability to punch, kick, or grab him. Once these factors are established, the spiritual warrior seeks a way to effectively disable his opponent with the least chance of personal damage. This way of penetrating an opponent's defenses is called the circle and the gate.

The circle encompasses an opponent's body. You need to find a passageway through his primary circle to penetrate his defenses. This passage is called the gate.

What should you look for as a gate? First of all, an opening in your opponent's defenses. In most confrontations, the opponent is in constant motion. At some point there will be a time when he is not in the best defensive posture with his hands and arms, or he will be off balance. These are the signs the conscious martial artist looks for as an opening of the gate. The spiritual warrior takes advantage of these gaps in his opponent's defenses and either launches a powerful strike or moves in and manipulates his opponent's body.

Offensive Exercises

The best exercise for penetrating an opponent's gate is facing off with an opponent. Stand in ordinary fighting stance with your fists up at chest level

Figure 11a

Figure 11b

(figure 11a). Have your opponent remain stationary. In a confrontation, before your opponent has the opportunity to move from his position, you could easily step slightly toward his forward side and deliver a powerful punch to his face between his upheld fists. Additionally, one of the most rapidly penetrating offensive techniques in a fighting stance is to launch a front kick under his fists, striking to his groin or solar plexus (figures 11b and 11c).

Although any trained opponent is obviously not going to remain in a stag-

Figure 11c

nant position for more than a moment, these two examples are illustrations of how the circle and gate theory works. A moment of hesitation is a gate, and it is all one needs to launch an effective offensive strike against an adversary. The spiritual warrior learns, through practice, how to effectively open and move through an opponent's gate.

Opponent Energy Manipulation

Martial artists train themselves to defend against any type of attack. These defenses traditionally take on the form of hard, forceful, traditional blocks against powerful punches and kicks. By blocking attacks forcefully, you may well stop an oncoming aggressive technique, but in doing so you may also damage your own body, be it a hand, arm, or forearm. It has been proven time and time again in street confrontations and professional competitions alike that by meeting force with force, bone to bone, the person who is deliberately blocking a very powerful offense will often damage part of her own body. There is, however, an effective method of defense from the onslaught of an assailant's attack, without the need of a forceful block. That method is called opponent energy manipulation.

Opponent energy manipulation allows you to take control of your opponent's own forward-moving energy and use it against him. This is accomplished by never forcefully encountering it.

By manipulating your opponent's

Figure 12a

energy as a primary tool of defense, you not only lessen the chances of being injured, but you also gain substantial control over your opponent's physical movements. You simply allow your opponent to make all the initial aggressive actions. Then, once these actions have been instigated, you simply guide his fighting techniques away from your body, using his own momentum.

Deflection

At the root of this method is the art of deflection. When you deflect you never forcefully encounter or block the assaults of an aggressor. Instead, you simply intercept the energy of his attack and redirect it to your own advantage. This forces your opponent to continue forward uncontrollably. The simplest example of this is, when an attacker rushes toward you (figure 12a), simply sidestep his attack as he approaches and give him a slight shove in the back or extend a foot to trip him (figures 12b and 12c). His momentum forces him to continue forward with his already expended energy and he easily is sent to the ground (figures 12d and 12e). By defending yourself in this fashion, you use little of your own energy and instead, take advantage of the already expended energy of your opponent.

Deflection is your best reaction to every assault. The art of deflection works because you allow your opponent's own aggressive momentum to continue moving him in the direction he originally intended. The only

Figure 12b

Figure 12c

Figure 12d

Figure 12e

Figure 13a

Figure 13b

difference between his intention and yours is that you don't allow his strike to make contact.

A simple exercise in opponent deflection has you actually do nothing at all to intercept or even touch your adversary once he has launched an aggressive attack at you. You simply move out of the way of any oncoming strike. For example, in the case of a straight punch, you would simply sidestep its path (figures 13a and 13b). From there, your opponent's expended energy causes him to continue forward,

Figure 13c

Figure 13d

Figure 13e

Figure 14a

Figure 14b

positioning him for your counterstrike (see, for example, figures 13c–13e).

In the event of a roundhouse punch or circular kick just step back out of its range (figures 14a and 14b). Your opponent's aggressive power forces him to continue the circular attack, leaving him vulnerable to your counterassault (see, for example, figures 14c–14e). In either case, these attempted strikes do not harm you, for you have neither received the impact of the hit nor have you forcefully intercepted it with a blocking technique. Although moving

Figure 14c

Figure 14d

Figure 14e

out of the way of oncoming attacks will give you superior counterattack positioning, avoidance generally is not enough to win a confrontation. Your opponent may instantly launch a powerful secondary attack at you if you do not immediately dominate his movements. For this reason, it is fundamental to the spiritual warrior to practice the theory of continuous motion in any physical altercation.

CONTINUOUS MOTION

The theory of continuous motion consists of five primary principles:

1. Always follow one technique with another.
2. Once your opponent has instigated the confrontation, you must assume that he has negative intentions in mind—do not give him the chance to launch a second attack.
3. Each defensive and offensive technique you perform must permit you to easily and effectively follow with another technique.
4. Always strike to the most accessible debilitating target on your opponent.
5. Never stop your attack until your opponent is completely subdued.

According to the theory, you move immediately from one technique, be it offensive or defensive, onto the next. As was illustrated in the examples of deflection, the moment the offensive technique missed its target is the time to launch effective countermeasures.

It is common for a defender to block or deflect an attack and then wait to see what the aggressor's next move will be. By allowing your attacker to define when and if a second attack will be launched, you allow him to dominate the altercation. For this reason, once a fight is imminent, it is up to you to set the boundaries and never let an opponent launch a second attack upon you. You do this by dominating the opponent once he launches a first strike attack, deflecting and then striking him in the most debilitating way with your ki energy.

If you choose to simply defend against an opponent's constant attacks, you will eventually be hit, which may result in your losing the confrontation. For this reason, if there is no other way around coming to physical blows, it is to your advantage to strike him powerfully before he can overpower you.

The theory of continuous motion

does not mean that you and your opponent go at it randomly, throwing whatever technique comes to mind, which is generally the case in many a street fight. With this type of fighting strategy you will both end up grappling like school children on the ground. The theory of continuous motion dictates that you understand what type of technique effectively follows your last movement. This is why the spiritual warrior continues his physical training and his spiritual development, because through practiced altercations the spiritual warrior safely learns what technique works best to defend against specific attacks and what technique efficiently follows another.

DEFENSE LEADING TO OFFENSE

Once you understand why continuous motion is important, you can integrate this theory with the art of deflection.

The first priority of a deflection defense is to witness the type of attacking movement your opponent is launching at you. His method of attack will directly influence which type of deflection and counterattack is most appropriate.

Linear movements, such as a straight punch, a push, a knife stab, or a straight front kick, due to their very linear nature, are best dealt with by initially sidestepping and thus moving out of the way of their oncoming impact. To illustrate this point more clearly, we can study the correct deflection procedure for the straight punch.

Your opponent attempts a straight punch at you (figure 15a). First, you sidestep the punch, out of harm's way (figure 15b). Simultaneously, you perform an in-to-out forearm deflection against your adversary's outstretched arm. By sidestepping and deflecting the punch, you keep your opponent's energy moving forward, something that a forceful block will never achieve. At the same time, you have kept his attacking arm held in check, so he cannot immediately launch a secondary attack at you. Therefore, you have achieved initial self-defense.

As discussed, deflection of an opponent's attack is never enough to assure victory in a confrontation. Therefore, once your deflection is performed, you must powerfully counterstrike or disable your opponent before he has the opportunity to launch a secondary attack at you.

In the case of the previously described straight punch attack, once it has been sidestepped and deflected, you see that with no further movement on your part, the physical motion your

Figure 15a

Figure 15b

adversary has instigated with the attack has him continuing to move forward until he is virtually touching you, body to body. From this position, there are very effective counterattacks. The simplest of these is a low side kick to his knee (figures 15c and 15d).

Much more common in street altercations is the circular attack. This is characterized by the wildly thrown roundhouse punch. Stepping back out of the way of this type of attack will cause the punch to miss you but that is rare, as an opponent who uses this

Figure 15c

Figure 15d

attack is generally going to continue throwing wild roundhouse punches until they begin to make contact. Therefore, we must view the elements that make up the roundhouse punch so we can learn how to effectively encounter this form of attack.

It begins at shoulder level and is thrown first outward and then in toward its target. The power of the roundhouse punch is developed from the momentum gained in its outward swing.

As an astute martial artist, you can take advantage of the relatively slow

Figure 16a

speed and obvious target of the round-house punch by initially stepping in toward your opponent slightly inside the punch's actual intended impact point (figure 16a). By doing this, the punch is rendered much less powerful, as it must be redirected to make contact. From this inside position, you can easily intersect your opponent's arm at his elbow level with an in-to-out knife hand interception (figure 16b).

By stepping in and simultaneously intercepting the roundhouse punch at your opponent's elbow, you have virtually taken control of your opponent's entire punching technique and body motion. Once you have intercepted the punch, you must immediately grab hold of his shoulder with the same hand you are deflecting with (figure 16c). This

will help you to control your opponent's movements and allows you easy manipulation of his momentum. From there, you can easily pivot on your feet and swing your assailant out and around your body. This movement is driven by your opponent's own momentum.

At this point in your roundhouse punch deflection defense, you will have not only thrown your opponent off balance but will have opened him up for a successful counterattack. The ideal counterstrike is a knife hand to the throat or across the nose of your opponent (figure 16d).

Deflection is effective when you take advantage of whatever part of your opponent's body you can use to our own advantage. This may be an extended

Figure 16b

Figure 16c

Figure 16d

Figure 16e

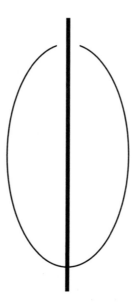

The Vertical Pathway

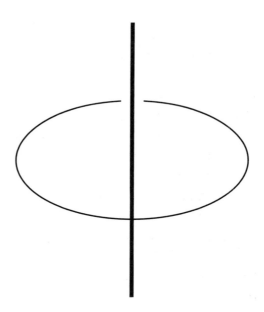

The Horizontal Pathway

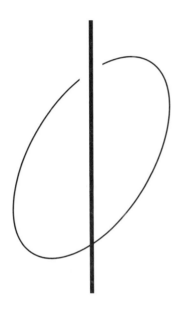

The Diagonal Pathway

foot—which you can trip—an out stretched arm—that once deflected, can be grabbed and then used to manipulate the opponent into the desired joint lock or throw, and so on.

THE THREE PATHWAYS OF GRAVITY

There are three pathways of gravity that the spiritual warrior uses in association with deflection to rapidly neutralize attacking opponents. They are the vertical, the horizontal, and the diagonal pathways (illustrated on this and the preceding page). These three pathways of gravity are instrumental in knocking an opponent off of his axis.

By understanding the three pathways of gravity, you allow yourself to rapidly take control over an opponent's forward attack motion and send him to the ground with the use of his own expended energy.

The Vertical Pathway

To efficiently utilize one of the three pathways of gravity, you simply direct an attacking opponent through the pathway that lies directly in their path of attack energy. For example, if an opponent attempts an overhead club strike at you, initially you would side-step slightly out of the path of the oncoming club (figure 17b). Thus, you are initially safe. Once the club strike has missed its target, most likely your head, you would immediately reach in and take hold of your attacker's forearm while it is still in motion (figure 17c). By allowing the force of the intended strike to continue through with its own preset direction, you would then guide his arms unnaturally behind his back (figure 17d). You then guide his arm farther behind his back, forcing his body to the ground (figures 17e and 17f). From this position, additional self-defense can be applied as necessary.

Figure 17a

Figure 17b

Figure 17c

Figure 17d

Figure 17e

Figure 17f

Figure 18a

Figure 18b

The Horizontal Pathway

A horizontal pathway attack may be observed in the launching of a linear knife stab. To defend against this, you would, as discussed, initially sidestep the knife's assault (figure 18b). Then, by taking hold of your opponent's wrist as it passes by your side, you would allow his forward-driven energy to keep moving as you pivot in a circular direction (figures 18c and 18d). This causes his forward motion to be controlled by you. By maintaining control of his wrist, you extend your leg (figure 18e) and trip him as his motion continues forward and is sent to the ground (figures 18f and 18g).

Figure 18c

Figure 18d

Figure 18e

Figure 18f

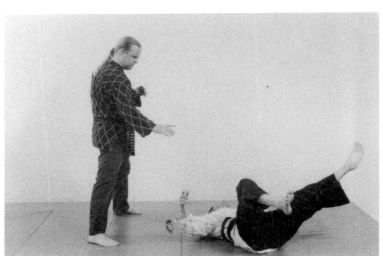

Figure 18g

Figure 19a

Figure 19b

The Diagonal Pathway

The diagonal pathway is ideally utilized when an opponent attempts to punch at your head (figure 19a). As he begins his attack, you rapidly step inside his punch by pivoting on your left foot and angling your body to a sideways-facing position (figure 19b). As you move in, you simultaneously take control of his forearm by grabbing it—left hand to right punching arm (figure 19c). Once in control, you instantly step deeper across his body, placing your shoulder under his punching arm. You continue his forward motion by launching him

Figure 19c

Figure 19d

over your shoulder, sending him to the ground (figures 19c and 19d).

These three basic examples of taking control of your opponent's three pathways of gravity give you an idea of how to isolate the pathways and determine which pathway is most appropriate. By taking advantage of the pathways of gravity, you not only minimize your attacker's impact on you but you also use very little energy in accomplishing your own self-defense.

ULTIMATE SELF-DEFENSE

The key element to continually successful opponent self-defense is to always use the opponent's own energy against himself. The spiritual warrior understands that it serves no purpose to fight an attacking opponent, strength against strength, when it is so simple to allow your adversary to expend all of his energy, while you save yours. To successfully achieve this energy matrix, you must take control and position yourself both in terms of the environment and in relation to your opponent, at the outset of any physical confrontation.

In confrontational situations, your opponent will generally attack you from the front. This, of course, is to your advantage, as you can witness your opponent's oncoming actions and effectively deflect them. In the event that you are attacked from the side or the back, it is to your advantage to disengage any hold your opponent may have on you and pivot to meet him head on, so no more surprise attacks can be launched at you. Although effective deflection can be achieved either from a rear or side attack, it is always easier if you can see an oncoming attack instead of having to guess what may or may not be in your opponent's mind.

With partner practice drills, executed in a freestyle sparring fashion, you will begin to learn what type of deflection is truly effective against the different types of attacks your opponent may launch at you. Through this practice, you will come to see how simple it is to overcome a much stronger opponent simply by allowing him to do all of the work, while your movements remain flowing and do not become stiff and stagnant. From this deepened understanding of deflection techniques, you will not only avoid unnecessary injury but you will also win the physical confrontations you encounter.

Physical combat is never desired, but it may sometimes be necessary. This is why the spiritual warrior chooses to refine her fighting techniques to the most precise physical movements possible. This way, she can maintain respect for all human life as well as protect her own.

AFTERWORD

No one can teach a person how to become a warrior. Fighting lessons can be given, confrontational techniques can be explained, but battle can never truly be described. It can only be understood through experience.

The martial artist enters a path of physical development in order to learn refined fighting techniques. He undertakes this training understanding that confrontation is at its core. It is not, however, until the martial artist is faced with actual physical engagement that he can appreciate what the implications of all-out war truly are.

Just as no one can teach you to be a physical warrior, no one can make you become a spiritual warrior. It is a personal choice. No one can lead you on the path of spiritual mastery through the martial arts. What you do with the information available to you is completely your choice.

The martial artist who chooses to rise above the lower levels of physical fighting skills and ascend, through his physical training, to a higher understanding is the one who becomes the spiritual warrior. The spiritual warrior follows a path of physical discipline and development, which actually leads her away from the need for physical confrontation. He consciously embraces the divine; thus, battle never has a need to find him.

Spiritual mastery is never easy. It takes much more time and personal application than physical development does. Spiritual mastery, however, is the path we are all on. Some of us simply do not choose to believe it. To this end, take the information in this book and use it as it applies to your life. Once on the spiritual path you will encounter numerous other beings who are moving in the same direction, and you will find many new sources for inspiration and spiritual development.

BIBLIOGRAPHY

Choy, Bong Young. *Korea: A History.* Rutland: Tuttle, 1971.

Chung, Kyung Cho. *New Korea: New Land of the Morning Calm.* New York: MacMillan, 1962.

Dening Esler. *Japan.* New York: Praeger, 1960.

Dumoulin, Heinrich. *Zen Buddhism: A History: India and China.* New York: Macmillan, 1988.

———. *Zen Buddhism: A History: Japan.* New York: Macmillan, 1990.

Fairbanks, John King. *China: A New History.* London: Belknap Press, 1992.

Giles, Lionel, Trans. *Sun Tzu: The Art of War.* Taipei: Taiwan Press, 1952.

Grayson, James Huntly. *Korea: A Religious History.* Oxford: Cavender Press, 1989.

Hall, Robert King, Ed. *Kokutai No Hungi: Cardinal Principals of the National Entity of Japan.* Newton: Crouton, 1974.

Han, Woo Kevin. *The History of Korea.* Seoul: Eul-Yoo, 1970.

Henthorn, William E. *A History of Korea.* New York: The Free Press, 1971.

Ikegami, Eiko. *The Taming of the Samurai: Honorific Individualism and the Making of Modern Japan.*

Cambridge: Harvard Univ. Press, 1995.

Kashiwahara, Yusen, and Koyu Sonoda, Eds. *Shapers of Japanese Buddhism*. Tokyo: Kosei, 1994.

Kim, Han Kyo, Ed. *Studies on Korea: A Scholar's Guide*. Honolulu: Univer. of Hawaii Press, 1980.

Kitagawa, Joseph M., and Mark D. Cummings, Eds. *Buddhism and Asian History*. New York: Macmillian, 1987.

Lee, Ki-baik. *A New History of Korea*. Cambridge: Harvard Univ. Press, 1984.

Lee, Peter H., Ed. *Source Book of Korean Civilization*. New York: Columbia Univ. Press, 1993.

Lee, Peter H., and Theodore De Barry, Eds. *Sources of Korean Tradition*. New York: Columbia Univ. Press, 1997.

Legge, James, Trans. *The Four Books*. Oxford: Univ. of Oxford Press, 1861.

Merrill, John. *Korea: The Peninsular Origins of War*. Newark: Univ. of Delaware Press, 1989.

Nahm, Andrew C. *Korea: Tradition and Transformation; A History of the Korean People*. Detroit: Western Michigan Univ. Press, 1988.

Rutt, Richard, Ed. *James Scarth Gale and His History of Korea*. Seoul: Tae Won, 1972.

Sato, Hiroaki. *Legends of the Samurai*. Woodstock: The Overlook Press, 1995.

Schwartz, Benjamin I. *The World of Thought in Ancient China*. Cambridge: Harvard Univ. Press, 1985.

Smith, Robert, and Beardsley, Richard K., Eds. *Japanese Culture: Its Development and Characteristics*. Chicago: Aldine, 1962.

Turnbull, S. R. *The Samurai: A Military History*. New York: Macmillan, 1977.

Veith, Iza, Trans. *The Yellow Emperor's Classic of Internal Medicine*. Berkley: Univ. of California Press, 1949.

Wakabayshi, Bob Tadashi. *Anti-foreignism and Western Learning in Early Japan*. Cambridge: Harvard Univ. Press, 1986.

INDEX